THE OCTAGON TECHNIQUE

AND OTHER LIFE LESSONS FROM COLLEGE

by

MICHAEL RUBIN MD

ISBN: 1466461004
ISBN 13: 9781466461000

THE OCTAGON TECHNIQUE

TECHNIQUE

AND OTHER LIFE LESSONS FROM COLLEGE

Thank you to my cousin Lisa.

For Mom and Dad. Thank you for making years

of university education available to me.

The Octagon Technique is a compilation of letters from

Mike's popular blog "The Rubin Review."

TABLE OF CONTENTS

INTRODUCTION

My bags are packed, I'm ready to go. I leave early tomorrow morning to begin the next phase of my educational journey as a college student at Eastern University in Ithaca, New York. I should probably be sleeping, but I have just spent the last hour tossing and turning in my bed wondering what the next few days, months and years have in store for me.

I am a little apprehensive. Leaving home, my family, and friends for three years is no easy decision. Luckily, we live in an age where we have the means to stay connected. I intend to keep you all fully updated on my day-to-day antics, and I hope you will do the same. After all, what's the point of humor and stupidity if you don't share the experiences with your friends?

It turns out, I am not the only one feeling sentimental about my departure. My leaving has taken a major toll on my parents. Over the last weeks they have been scrambling to ensure that I have everything I need and that they have completed teaching me everything I must know to fend for myself.

Today, I received the last and final installment of this training.

"Michael, we will be going to the pharmacy to buy your toiletries at noon, don't forget to make a list," my mother reminded me, as I packed my clothing into the suitcase.

I could tell she was up to something. She only calls me "Michael" when she is either mad at me or preparing me for a serious talk. Not to mention that had been the third time she reminded me of our outing, since I woke up that morning.

"What's going on, Mom? Is there something bothering you?" I asked.

"Well, now that you mention it, there is one item your father and I wanted to chat with you about," she began. "Michael, you are now a young adult, old enough to move out and live on your own... Living on your own will impart new freedoms and more privacy. There will be opportunities to explore and try new things. You have to be responsible and make good decisions. Basically, I want you to think with your head, not with your...'shmeck.' You always have to take precautions."

"Mom, don't start with me. I'm old enough to take care of myself."

"Well, I just want you to think ahead; you always need to be prepared... Do you have any 'SAFES' for school?"

I was speechless. "You know, CONDOMS?" she added. The word "condom" seemed to float through the air like a giant hot air balloon.

"Oh God, nooo!" I yelled. I couldn't believe she had just asked me that. I was mortified.

"We'll pick some up later when we go to the pharmacy to buy your toiletries," she answered.

I tried everything to wriggle out of the trip to the pharmacy but with my mom, there is no wriggling out of anything. My one hope was that she would forget and save us both the embarrassment of buying "safes." I could only imagine how humiliating it would be standing next to my mom at the cash register, as the clerk rang the box of condoms into the register.

In the pharmacy near our house, the condom section is situated immediately after the shampoo aisle. There is no avoiding it. It just so happens to be in the most exposed area of the pharmacy. It is in clear view of the pharmacist, the prescription waiting area, and right beside the public blood pressure machine.

As I picked out my shampoo, I realized the wall of condoms lay ahead. *Maybe if I push the shopping cart up the aisle quickly my mother won't notice the thousands of colorful condom boxes.*

I scurried up the aisle to scout the area. There was an elderly couple checking their blood pressure on the sphygmomanometer, as well as a group of people waiting for their prescriptions. Luckily, there was no one I knew. I had managed to turn the corner and thought I was in the clear when I heard my mother call out: "Michael, come back here…you have to pick one."

"I'm not coming back," I answered.

"Michael, get over here, *now*. Do not make a scene." Somehow I felt there was going to be a scene no matter what.

I decided I would pick the first box I saw and stifle the ordeal quickly before the surrounding spectators could tune in to what was going on.

I grabbed the first neon box that caught my eye, threw it into the shopping cart and urged my mother to move on.

She picked up the box and looked at my selection. "Glow in the dark condoms…? You want to use fluorescent glow in the dark condoms? The girl is going to laugh at you!" my mother blurted out as she examined the box.

The old couple at the sphygmomanometer clued in to what was going on.

I grabbed the next box that caught my eye. Again, it didn't pass my mother's approval.

"What do you need flavored condoms for?" she laughed.

"I don't know, Mom, I'm just picking anything to make this stop! Can we please move on?"

The aisle seemed to have every kind of prophylaxis except for the regular type. My next selection had huge bulbous studs, which my mother didn't approve of either.

I was so embarrassed, I wanted to lie down and run the shopping cart over my throat. The old couple at the sphygmomanometer found the ordeal quite humorous and continued to take their blood pressure an additional five or six times so they could inconspicuously stay and watch.

Finally, I just grabbed a variety pack. There were six different types in the package; surely one of them would meet her approval…

"Oh, my God…how much sex are you planning on having?" she yelled accusingly.

"Mom, every type I choose is no good. Why don't you just pick for me? Which type do you and *Dad* use?"

That turned things around a little. Now she was equally as embarrassed. The old man's arm turned blue from a lack of circulation, but he didn't mind. He was laughing hysterically.

"That's it, I'm going to go ask the pharmacist," my mother threatened.

A short old lady in a lab coat came out to help us.

"My son will be having sex for the first time, can you recommend a brand of condom for him?"

"Mom, how would you know that?" I protested.

"Michael, is there something you want to tell me?" she asked.

The pharmacist stared me up and down a couple of times, as if to make a conclusion on her own, and focused for a second on my crotch area.

She picked up two boxes of ordinary condoms and gave me the option: "With or without spermicidal lubricant...I recommend using spermicide for additional protection...and don't worry, it's one size fits all," she said in her raspy old woman voice.

I have no doubt that I am going to miss my family, but I am excited for the much-needed independence. Although I can hardly imagine there will be any privacy in my on-campus student residence. From what I understand, my dorm room is the size of a shoebox, and I have to share it with a roommate.

I guess I should enjoy my last couple of hours of sleep in my own private room. As of tomorrow night, I will be sharing my life with a complete stranger.

Goodnight,

Mikey

SEMESTER 1 LETTER 1

My dorm is known as the "Zoo," and it couldn't have a more appropriate name. It is huge and wild and smells like animal! Statistically, it is comprised of 1252 students on twenty-seven floors, making it the second largest residence in North America. The Zoo has the infamous reputation of being the party epicenter of campus. Many people come and hang out here just for the residence's social atmosphere.

I am adjusting well. The school has a ratio of three females for every two males. This pleases me. There should be a total of twenty-six thousand undergraduate students here by the time classes begin later this week. The possibilities seem endless. I think I am going to love my new university playground!

My classes this semester include chemistry, biochemistry, human physiology, ecology, and lab. Already, I can tell that university is nothing like high school. Some professors don't even want to speak with students and only lecture because they need university funding for their research.

Let me note how independent I have become. I have shopped for food (real groceries), and I do my own laundry. (Actually, a female neighbor helped me a little the first time.) I have already managed to wash (and ruin) my student validation card, bus pass, and health insurance card, which is a real pain because they are important. I had to wait in a long line to get them replaced.

I have been attending tryouts for the university wrestling team. I don't know if I can make the time commitment to wrestle varsity, but the school holds its athletes in high esteem. I have been attending all six try-outs a week, as well as the early morning jogs. The university sports teams are big here, and it is a real honor to be awarded a varsity position. I don't know if I have the time or energy to be a student athlete, but for now, I'm getting into amazing shape.

THE FRATERNITY RUSH

Yesterday, I ran into two guys I recognized from back home. They are both initiated fraternity brothers, and they persuaded me to check out their fraternity. Last night, I "rushed" The Modern Gentleman's Fraternity. It was a phenomenal experience. The activity was a "House Crawl," showcasing several sororities the fraternity socializes with.

At each sorority house, we were greeted by beautiful women, hors-d'oeuvres, and a selection of wine, beer, and liquor. At the second house, the hostess requested that we "entertain" two girls who had been study-ing all day long in the sorority library. We were blindfolded and led upstairs. Suddenly, dance music started playing, and one of the girls that welcomed us at the door began to undress me.

We were ordered to dance and, naturally, we attempted to give the girls an entertaining show. Once undressed, our blindfolds were removed. There were close to forty beautiful women sitting around the perimeter of the room ogling us. The ladies then approached us one by one to introduce themselves. If this was what fraternity life was like, I wanted in!

SEMESTER 1 LETTER 2

The Zoo is wild; there is always something crazy going on. Recently a goat was kidnapped from a local farm and released to wreak havoc on my floor. Today, the hallway on the fifth floor was completely covered with tarp, and a "Slip and Slide" was laid out the length of the hall. Everyone was in bikinis and bathing suits, rubbing shaving cream all over one another and hurling themselves down the hall on their stomachs.

While sliding, one of my neighbors got her bellybutton piercing caught on something and it ripped right out of her stomach. Now she has the two ugly "pincers" hanging out of her bellybutton. I figure she will probably have to get it fixed, unless bellybutton "tentacles" becomes a new fad.

University is all about decisions. At any time of the day, you can always find a party, a study group, or some form of organized athletic activity. What is difficult is defining the proper balance between responsible and irresponsible activities. I figure as long as my work is getting done and I'm not completely dead from wrestling, I will catch as much of the fun as possible.

THE STUDY MACHINE

Anna, one of my residence neighbors, has only one objective: to get the highest grades possible. She also happens to be gorgeous. She is an excellent person to study next to, because she works so damned hard and is such a pleasure to stare at. One day, we met at the entrance to the library, and I followed her to a study room. I sat next to her, and I figured that I would try to impress her by mimicking her study habits. I decided I wouldn't get up, go to the bathroom, or leave, unless she did first.

I was working really well, feeding off her discipline, until a massive young woman came storming into the study room. She trampled over everyone's bags and disrupted everyone as she tried to squeeze her immense torso through the tight seating spaces. Even once she found a cubicle she liked, she had to search for a new chair to better accommodate her huge ass. She let out a grunt or two and then began to work.

After a couple minutes, BIG BERTHA reached into her bag and took out an iPod. The volume was so loud that I could hear her music from where I was sitting. I was annoyed. I had been studying well, until BIG BERTHA came along and shattered my concentration. It seemed that with every little sniffle or grunt she made, it became harder and harder to focus. Nobody was more annoyed than Anna. With each disruption, she became exponentially more irritated.

Bertha proceeded to take a giant hole-puncher out of her bag. I didn't think she had the audacity to start hole punching in the "quiet zone" of the library but she did. PUNCH, PUNCH, and PUNCH, the sound echoed through the room. Looking around, I noticed everyone was irate. Even the guy next to me who had been comatose in his cubicle was awakened by the punching noise. The noise went on for what seemed like an eternity. As soon as BIG BERTHA's grubby fingers could collect enough papers, there came an imminent PUNCH sound. After each PUNCH there was a very obvious murmur of "shut the fuck up" coming from the surrounding cubicles. BIG BERTHA wasn't taking the hint. Suddenly, little Anna had had enough. She walked toward the beast, stood over the woman's obese frame, and tapped her shoulder.

"Would you mind not doing that in this room? We are trying to study." she said politely. Everyone stopped studying to watch.

"Oh, don't worry, I'm almost done," BIG BERTHA responded and continued organizing her next punch.

Anna prepared herself to give a punch of her own. "Stop now and get out!" It was at that exact moment that Anna became my hero. For the first time since BIG BERTHA had walked in, there was dead silence. I let out a "YOU TELL HER, GIRL," and soon the whole room was cheering. BIG BERTHA, embarrassed, waddled out of the study room a minute later.

The next day, there was a similar occurrence. Someone was playing cell phone games in the study room, and everyone in the vicinity was annoyed by the beeping sound. Inspired by Anna's previous success, I decided it was my turn to be the hero. I followed the noise and stood over the source cubical. (All the time reminding myself that I had recently been invited to compete on the university wrestling team.) Unfortunately, the guy playing the game was a huge, tattooed individual, probably named BUBBA. I gave him a little wave (pretending to think I mistook him for someone else) and scampered away as quickly as my legs could carry me.

WRESTLING TEAM ROOKIE INITIATION

Last night was the Varsity Wrestling Team initiation party. As a yearly ritual, the veteran team members brutally initiate the rookies. Upon entering the team house, all the rookies were given party hats. We were instructed to wear the hats the entire evening. If caught without it, we would be forced to chug beer until vomiting ensued. We were each given a cup of very sketchy beer that was specially prepared ahead of time. I suspect it contained a laxative, because in turn, each of us ended up having to wrestle one another to use the toilet. Then the team captain took out a shaver. One by one they grabbed rookies, pinned us down, and shaved us bald, leaving only a little Mohawk on the top of our heads. As the veterans became more inebriated, the shavings became more creative and certainly uglier.

As luck would have it, on one of my trips to the washroom, my party hat fell into the toilet. Some of the guys noticed me without it, and I was forced to suffer the consequence: a KEG STAND. I was held upside down over a beer keg. The hose was placed in my mouth and beer was pumped down my throat, until I barfed up my stomach contents. I survived the punishment with only minor aspirations.

We were then taken downtown, where we met up with all the other Eastern Varsity athletes. It was a lot of fun. I am honored to have been invited onto the varsity roster, but I know that balancing sports, studying, and a social life will be a challenge.

CULTURE SHOCK

For the past week, I have done nothing but study. Sometimes, if I remember, I will eat, but otherwise I study, study, study. My meals consist mainly of bottled water, Coke, chocolate-covered almonds, and peach jellies. I'm not lying when I say university is a fierce battle against scurvy.

My roommate Chan-Lee, an exchange student from Hong Kong, is in complete culture shock. He spends his weekends in the lab. In fact, last week he packed a suitcase and spent the entire week in the science lab. I literally didn't see the guy once from Thursday to Thursday. I told him that he was nuts but, quite frankly, I didn't mind having the room to myself. Once, when Chan-Lee came back from the lab, he slept for a couple of days and then woke up covering his ears and making the weirdest sounds. "NIEYYY, NIEYY." He then proceeded to run to the bathroom and throw up blood. The doctor gave him medication and several injections in his back. I thought that would have been a clear sign for him to stop going to the lab, but he still goes. I'm beginning to think "the lab" is a code word for something else.

SPARE A SQUARE

I have a phobia of public restrooms, always have. I am slowly becoming accustomed to the reality that I share a bathroom with every other guy on my floor. Whenever I use the toilet, I pad it with a minimum of fifty squares using my newly developed Octagon Technique. I carefully lay strips of toilet paper over the seat to form an eight-sided protective barrier between my ass and the putrid toilet seat.

The other day, I ate cafeteria fish for dinner...BIG MISTAKE! I was studying in the library when the fish, all of a sudden, decided it wanted out. When an event such as this happened before, I just packed up my stuff and ran back to the Zoo. This time, however, there was no time to run anywhere. I had to go—and fast. My only option was the library bathroom. I busted through the doors and into one of the most unsightly bathrooms I'd ever laid eyes on. There was paper on the ground and residue on the seats, along with a smell of paint masked by the pungent smell of excrement. It was an immediate assault on my olfactory senses. I didn't care. I felt like a ticking time bomb...I just wanted to be in the right place when I exploded. The toilet seats were filthy beyond covering. Even my Octagon Technique couldn't prevent disease. I decided to "hover" using one arm as a lever on the bottom of the stall door and the other arm as a support against the wall.

I felt like a coffee percolator. Liquid was pouring out of me like a tap. The guy in the stall next to me started laughing. I was mortified; I brought my feet closer together so he couldn't identify me by my shoes. I was so adamant about getting my business done that I had been oblivious to my surroundings. I hadn't noticed how dirty the floor was or the sign on the stall door that read "Careful, wet paint." Only when the bulk of the explosion had occurred and I repositioned my hands, did I realize they were covered in blue paint.

Instinctively, I started using the toilet paper to wipe my hands. Before long, I had used it all up. I thought about my options. I had no choice but to ask the guy in the stall next to me for help.

"Hey, Buddy, could you spare a square?"

The guy started laughing. "No problem, Dude...you might want to consider laying off the baby food."

I was humiliated, and I was at the mercy of some asshole who was making fun of me. He held a large wad of toilet paper under the stall. I reached for it with my blue hand, which sent him into a laughing frenzy. What the fuck...I may as well laugh too. I finished my business and waited in the stall until the guy left. Another shitty story!

It's been a couple of days and my hands still have a bluish tint, which leads me to believe my rear is also somewhat blue. I guess it's better that there is currently no girl in my life to have to explain this to.

SEMESTER 1 LETTER 3

THE HELIUM DISASTER

Last week there were elections for the Awards Commissioner position on the Science Student Council. Each candidate was required to give a one-minute speech in front of the entire Science Council. Then the Council would vote on which of the candidates merited the position. I figured the position was as good as mine...I'm usually quite good at addressing an audience. I wrote several versions of my speech, but I came to realize that one minute is too short to pass off any form of intelligent humor. I wanted to be funny yet informative at the same time...a truly challenging task given the time constraint. Then it occurred to me... instead of finding a balance between funny and informative, why not give a serious speech in a funny way? That's where the helium gas came in. It seemed like a novel idea at the time. I was sure the idea would stun the audience...and so it did, just not in the way I had hoped.

I searched around Ithaca for a small helium tank. All I found was a foot-high tank (the same size as the propane tanks for barbecues.) I figured it would look cooler sucking helium from a tank than from a balloon, so I rented it. The next step was to find some sort of piping that would bring the gas from the tank to my mouth. It just so happened that the campus pharmacy had an oxygen mask, which they gladly loaned me free of charge. It was a really cool set-up. I just had to turn on the tank, put on the mask and a couple of seconds later I would be speaking like Alvin the Chipmunk.

The elections were held in a large auditorium. I was the sixth candidate to speak. All the speeches before mine were mundane…they were all the same. "I was president of the student council…I this, I that; vote me because I'm the best guy." My speech was similar, only I was going to give it in a really high-pitched voice.

When I was called up, I brought my helium tank. Heads popped up, eyes opened wide…people had no idea what I was about to do. Just to be funny I asked if there was a medic in the room and suggested they come sit closer. I went into one of those surreal states when I am given the floor, and I'm anticipating getting a crowd laughing. Only this time, something went terribly wrong.

Everything happened very quickly, but I recall the events in slow motion. I brought the mask to my face and opened the tank valve. Before I knew it, helium was rushing into my lungs way too fast. My thorax expanded, my stomach bloated, and my eyes bulged out of their sockets. I pulled the mask off my face and stared, dazed, at the audience. The world seemed to be moving in slow motion. I remember seeing the time-keeper give me my cue to start. However, I just stared at the audience in total confusion and disorientation. After about ten seconds, I managed to regain control of myself. I picked up my speech but no sounds would come out of my mouth. Then there was a small high-pitched hiccup. I looked down at my distended stomach and knew exactly what was about to happen. There was no stopping it. 5…4…3…2…1 BLASTOFF! Gas came reverberating up my esophagus, resulting in the longest high-pitched burp EVER. The sound thundered through the auditorium. If we were in a cartoon, everybody would have been blown backwards out of their seats.

There was about a second's awkward pause, followed by blaring laughter. People were bellowing. In the squeakiest most high-pitched noise my body has ever mustered, I yelped, "Pardon me." I then introduced myself and stated the position I was running for. Before I was even able to give the opening line of my speech, the timekeeper yelled, "Time!," and I was forced to sit down.

It didn't come as a surprise when I wasn't voted onto the Science Council. Although people seemed to have enjoyed my speech, there just wasn't enough substance. Despite not being voted in, I have become quite the popular character with the Council. Maybe one day, "Helium Boy" will find his way into student politics.

SEMESTER 1 LETTER 4

CUTTING WEIGHT

I had my first wrestling tournament this weekend. Two weeks ago I weighed 155 lbs., which is a regular healthy weight for me. I weighed in for the tournament last Friday at exactly 143 lbs. That is a twelve-pound drop in weight in less than a week. I call it the "Mike Rubin Super Wrestling Diet." Please do not try this at home.

For the first part of the week, I just ate carefully…two meals a day… healthy food. Toward the end of the week, I stopped eating and drinking. Two hours before the weigh-in deadline, I was still eight pounds overweight. I had to lose eight pounds in less than two hours. I put on two pairs of pants, three shirts, a winter jacket and a hat, and ran for an hour in a sauna without drinking. I managed to sweat out nearly eight pounds of liquid. It was gross to say the least.

After the weigh-in, I was extremely weak. I stumbled back to the Zoo, ate a little, and passed out on my bed. I could have slept for days, but two hours into my slumber, Anna and a couple of girls barged into my room. I had promised them that I was going to go out partying with them. Even in my totally exhausted state, I couldn't say no to going out with five women, especially Anna.

I ended up at a downtown club with the five ladies. They all started drinking—heavily. I couldn't drink. I hadn't eaten a real meal in days, and the alcohol would have seared my stomach. We eventually made our way onto the dance floor, and despite my low energy levels, I attempted to dance. I was having fun until a couple of sketchy characters noticed that there was a crew of five inebriated women accompanied by only one male. Slowly, the guys crept closer and started dancing with my friends. It didn't bother me that the girls were being pegged off one by one, as long as I was dancing with Anna. It was only when one of the girls became "rag doll" drunk that I became concerned. She was barely able to stand, and an aggressive guy took full advantage of the opportunity to dance with her. She looked like she was having fun, so I just made sure to keep her in sight. At that point, three of the five girls had been picked up, and I felt like a police officer constantly patrolling to ensure they were all fine.

Eventually, the sleaze supporting the rag doll pulled a move. He held her close, placed his hands up her shirt and was forcing himself on her. She started panicking, but she was too weak to resist him. I was dead tired, worn out from a week of training while not eating. The last thing I wanted to do was start a bar fight. I had no choice; he was abusing one of my friends.

Within seconds, I had him in a headlock. If he tried to fight, I was going to throw him, and teach him a very painful lesson. Holding him in the lock, allowing only the bare minimum of blood to circulate through his carotid arteries, I ordered him to leave the girls alone. He left the bar and didn't come back, thus bestowing upon me hero status. I think Anna was impressed! All this training had made me a pretty confident fighter…except where it counts, on the mats.

RINGWORM

I had two days to regain all my weight before the tournament. You can only imagine how much I ate. The tournament was a disaster. My first match was against a Russian guy. I was warned that he was a Greco champion from Russia and that I should avoid "tying up" with him at all costs. I wasn't nervous at all. I believed I could potentially beat him.

I'll try and explain my thoughts through the fight, which only ended up lasting forty-five seconds. At first I was just thinking, "Don't tie up, don't tie up," but once the match began, I remember thinking, *Holy crap what is that awful smell? Don't tie up...avoid the pungent smell!* Then I started analyzing the smell. *Maybe this Russian dude likes garlic? Don't tie up to avoid the garlic smell.* Then he grabbed me and sucked my head deep into his armpit. At that point, my thoughts became clouded by the odor. *Maybe he eats asparagus and never showers?* I didn't care what happened next, as long as I escaped the smell. Then he tied me up and used some classic Greco Roman throw. Both of us flew through the air, and I landed on my left shoulder. I was no longer worried about the smell. My left arm went completely numb. He then pinned me, winning the match.

My trainer treated me for two hours so that I would be able to fight my next match. Before the match, she taped up the shoulder to keep it from dislocating. Rather than holding my shoulder together, the bandage served as a flag saying, "This is where it hurts." That match didn't last so long either.

I spent most of my week seeing doctors and getting x-rays and physiotherapy. This injury was, in a way, a blessing in disguise. Now that I was hurt, I had time to catch up with my studies. My coach seemed to have a very different outlook on my purpose as a university student. Whereas his objective was to groom me to be a world-class athlete, my goal was to be the best possible student. For me, academics would always trump athletics. For many of my teammates, wrestling had enabled their university education. For me, academics presented me with the opportunity to wrestle, but since I wanted to become a physician, I would never permit athletics to compromise my education.

I did however go to practice for an hour this last week to speak to the coach. At practice, I noticed that one of my teammates was wrestling wearing a full-body tracksuit. I was a little confused, because we only wrestled in suits when we were cutting weight, and since there was no competition I couldn't understand what he was doing. Then someone informed me that his body had been invaded by ringworm and that he was wearing the suit to keep it from spreading to other teammates. Ringworm is a parasitic organism that eats away at your skin. When I heard that, I was ecstatic that I was injured. I didn't want to go anywhere near the mats until that guy was cured or completely devoured.

٢

SEMESTER 1 LETTER 5

It's exam time here at Eastern and life is stressful. Most of the people around me have become nocturnal (sleep by day…study by night). I am looking forward to heading home for Christmas break. There is nothing I miss more than having a clean toilet seat to sit on. There is no such thing as privacy or personal space in the Zoo. Phyllis, our seventy-four-year-old superintendent, has a fascination with cleaning the men's washroom. She's always in there!

At the beginning of the semester, I was hesitant to shower while she was cleaning. Now I just wave to her and hop right in. The showers here are more like pressure washers. The sheer pressure of the water has put holes in my skin. I usually point the showerhead toward the wall and shower in the deflecting water. Unfortunately, this causes an air current within the shower that reveals my naked body without warning to everyone in the bathroom—including Phyllis.

The temperature of the water is also temperamental. Whenever someone flushes one of the toilets, there is an immediate ten-degree jump in water temperature. Considering the small size of the showers, the only way to escape the scalding-hot water is to thrust my body against the shower wall. (It's not something I think about…it's a reflex.) I find it funny that as soon as someone flushes the toilet I can expect to hear a series of thuds followed by howls coming from the showers.

THE SNOW WAR

Last night, I desperately wanted a good night's sleep. I finished studying and made all the necessary preparations to be in bed by midnight. My roommate Chan-Lee had other plans. He was hacking away at his computer. Who can sleep in a room when someone is typing and their screen brightens the whole room? By 1:30 a.m., I was fed up! I kindly gave him the option of going to sleep or going out the window. He chose sleep.

At three in the morning, I woke up to a blaring alarm. Chan-Lee was standing over my bed holding my alarm clock and frantically pressing buttons. I quickly realized the noise wasn't coming from the clock. The fire alarm was ringing. Chan-Lee was freaking out; he had been in the lab the last time the fire alarm went off in our dorm and probably thought we were under attack.

I quickly calmed him down and told him to go back to bed. This was the third time the alarms had sounded in the middle of the night that month. There was no chance I was evacuating this time. We lay in our beds with the siren echoing. We could hear the fire trucks and all the people evacuating their rooms and collecting outside behind the building. I refused to leave...not this time. I needed a good night's sleep!

Soon we heard the sound of Darth Vader's heavy breathing. A slew of firemen were walking around our floor in fire suits and gas masks. Two firefighters barged through our door, grabbed Chan-Lee and carried him out. I quickly put on all my warmest clothing and bolted down the fire escape.

Apparently, people learned a valuable lesson during the last fire alarm. Everyone was dressed in warm clothing...no naked people this time. It was 3:30 in the morning and there were some fourteen hundred people hanging out on a snowy basketball court behind the Zoo. The firemen distributed blankets in hopes that everyone would huddle together to keep warm.

Then it started...All it took was a single snowball for people to realize that the snow was the perfect consistency for a snowball fight. The snowballs started multiplying exponentially and people retreated to both ends of the basketball court. In a matter of seconds the mob of fourteen hundred people was divided into two distinct camps at either end of the court. The sky was filled with thousand of snowballs, and commanders arose on both teams. The blankets—intended to keep us warm—were collected and stretched to serve as shields. Thousands of snowballs were flying in every direction. It looked like a medieval war scene. One poor guy ended up at center court and was bombarded by snowballs from both sides. It truly was an amazing sight.

As much as I wanted to let loose and participate, I knew I had to find a place to sleep. I ended up walking to my friend Sammy's residence. Fortunately, she welcomed me in and let me sleep on the end of her bed like a little dog.

SANTA MATCH

The captain of the wrestling team threw a Christmas party at the team house. At practice we had to pick a name out of a hat for a gift exchange. The rule was that the gift had to be liquor.

The wrestling team has a tradition that is honored every Christmas season. The largest heavyweight on the team (this year, it was a guy named Teddy) dresses up as Santa and distributes the gifts one by one. Imagine Teddy, a two hundred and forty-five-pound Santa, sitting in a big chair with the varsity wrestling team sitting all around him. When your name is called, you have to go up and sit on Teddy's lap and open your gift. Seeing as all the presents are booze, you are expected to drink as much as you can in one chug. Santa/Teddy then has to "match" whatever amount you drank.

The first person up, the team medic, got the gift I bought, a small bottle of Baileys chocolate liquor. The medic sucked down half the bottle in one chug; so naturally, Santa had to finish it. During the party Teddy managed to take a swig from at least twenty-five different alcoholic beverages without even showing the slightest sign of intoxication.

I was warned, however, that the tradition is not complete unless Santa pukes by midnight. I was shocked that even a big guy could stomach such a variety of liquors without puking, let alone going into a coma. Then the captain of the wrestling team was called up. The captain, who is no small guy himself, went to sit on Santa's lap. Someone had become overly creative with the captain's gift: a bottle of Captain Morgan rum, a box of Captain Crunch cereal and a package of Captain Highliner

Fish Sticks. After polishing off the rum, the captain moved on to the box of fish sticks. He started scarfing down raw fish patties. It looked repulsive! Naturally Santa had to match whatever was consumed. We all started chanting, "SANTA MATCH, SANTA MATCH!"

Teddy started shoveling the raw fish patties down his throat. He was fighting the urge to gag; regurgitation was imminent! Several seconds after eating his last raw fish patty, Teddy stood up abruptly. He shot a dazed stare across the room. His eyes rolled back into his head, and he made a mad dash for the bathroom. Only he fell on the way and barfed all over the walls. (Apparently this happens every year.) People were cheering. What a wonderful time of the year.

SEMESTER 2 LETTER 1

DEHYDRATION

I have finally accepted a "bid" of acceptance into a fraternity. My life is now partitioned three ways: school, wrestling, and fraternity. With all the "cutting weight" that I have done in the last two weeks, eating just hasn't been part of my daily routine. Life has been a constant struggle with *manorexia*.

Last week, I had to cut serious weight for a wrestling competition. I fear I may have put myself into acute kidney failure. I was simultaneously trying to study for exams. I figured that it was pointless to study when I was so dehydrated, so I drank liquids up until the day of my weigh-in. Then I spent hours jogging in a snowsuit in the sauna. When I finally went into the weigh-in, my hands looked like prunes and every drop of moisture had been sucked out of my lips and mouth.

It wasn't even worth my while to cut weight. The competition was here at Eastern, and many wrestlers came up from other colleges to compete. My first match was against the U.S. champion from the Michigan State team. I was glad the match didn't last too long. I don't remember much of what happened, but I do remember being picked up by my legs and swung around in circles only to be released to fly halfway across the mat. A couple of my friends came to watch the match; they even made me a "GO MIKE GO" sign, which is the only thing I remember seeing as I was being spun in circles.

My next fight was my best fight of the year. I went in tough and scored six points before the guy was able to touch me. Toward the end of the match, the guy got me all tangled up. Apparently, it was hard to tell where my body ended and my opponent's body began…a move that nobody gets out of…except for me!

After the fight, the coach asked me, "How in God's name did you get out of that hold?" I explained that for a couple of seconds I was defenseless. "Extreme situations call for extreme measures. There was a crotch right in front of my face, so I bit it…" There is no telling what you can do when you bite your own nuts!

SEMESTER 2 LETTER 2

I have now been formally initiated into The Modern Gentleman's Fraternity. Since the traditions, principles, and ideals of most fraternities remain within the "brotherly bond," I am not at liberty to divulge any of the events or rituals that constituted my initiation. All I can say is that initiation week was the most fun I *never* want to have again. But, alas, now I can reap the full benefits of being an initiated fraternity member. I can say there is probably some truth to the fraternity initiations portrayed in movies…minus the goat.

I have also received an award from the University Residence Council. I have somehow been deemed "the student with the healthiest lifestyle." I find this extremely ironic, given my starvation diet. It's no nuclear physics award, but at least I have been singled out as a role model for something.

THE VARSITY BANQUET

Last night, I attended the Varsity Athletics Banquet. Eastern rented a hall in town and hosted a formal dinner for all the varsity athletes. There were at least two thousand athletes in the hall, who play every sport from pole-vaulting to football. The event started in the afternoon and most of the athletes showed up drunk. Bottles of wine were being passed around like water and, before long, the football players were hitting on the figure skaters, the squash players were arguing with the tennis players, and the female rugby players were making out with each other. The crowd was so noisy and wild that the Athletics Department was barely able to present the awards.

After dinner, dancing broke out. All the teams rushed to the dance floor and claimed their territory. I spent a couple of minutes dancing with the wrestling chicks, but since they are not my type, I ventured deeper into the mob on the dance floor. A few steps out of wrestling territory, I found myself surrounded by very burly, buff women, most of whom had the "mushroom cut." They were the notorious women's rugby team and were too busy feeling up the girls beside them to notice me. I walked another couple of steps, until I was surrounded by tree-like people; surprise, surprise, I had entered the realm of the basketball players. Another couple of steps and finally the girls looked decent. They were slim, well defined, and they all had a full set of teeth. It took a couple of seconds before I realized they all had huge biceps and the muscular, triangular-shaped back that only avid swimmers possess. I eventually ended up dancing alongside the female cheerleaders whom I found to be the most attractive.

THE GNOME

For my birthday, Sammy bought me a garden gnome. Let me just say that it was one of the best presents I have ever received.

I was sitting at my desk and decided to take a break from studying to send her a special thank-you e-mail for the gift. Using animation software on my computer, I used my web cam to animate the gnome. I made a short video of the gnome moving around my desk.

Just as I was about to e-mail the clip to Sammy, my neighbor Maggie walked into my room. Proud of my creation, I decided to show her the clip. I figured she would be impressed by my animating skills. Only instead of congratulating me on my abilities, she totally flipped out: "Oh my God, the gnome is alive! AAAAHHH AAAHHH get it away!"

Realizing the opportunity for an amazing practical joke, I immediately began to fake a panic as well: "I know it's alive...it moves whenever I leave my room. For days now someone has been messing up my desk...and I know it's not Chan-Lee because he has been in the lab for nine days."

I explained to Maggie that I had set the motion detector on my computer to see who was coming into my room and messing up my desk... and all I got was a short video of the gnome moving around. We decided that we would leave the motion detector on while we went down to dinner to see if we could detect any further activity.

I came up from dinner early without her noticing and quickly put together another set of animations. Once again, I made a clip of the gnome roaming around my desk, moving things telekinetically and staring into the camera in a "threatening" manner. By the time Maggie made her way to my room, I had worked myself into another "panic."

I showed her the clips and she turned white as a ghost. She wanted to tell the world...

"We must call the police," she insisted.

I refused, saying, "We alone have to get to the bottom of it." I had managed to work myself up to the point where my hands were trembling and goose bumps were developing on my arms. *I should have won an Academy Award.* After some time, she decided to approach the gnome and pick it up. Don't think I didn't give a blood-curdling yelp as soon as she finally touched it.

I had done such a good job pretending to be frightened that I actually started to share in her anxiety. But then again, I figured that if she was gullible enough to believe in such a ridiculous situation she deserved to learn a lesson.

That night, I was sleeping peacefully, when I heard a rumbling on my desk. I quickly glanced around the room. Obviously the noise was not coming from Chan-Lee; he was in the lab. I looked across the room at my desk only to see the little green gnome staring back at me. I was petrified! I hid under my covers hoping that it was all just my imagination. Then I heard the noise again...a violent sound coming from my desk where the gnome was perched. I was very frightened and readied myself to be attacked. Another couple of seconds went by, and the horrid thumping continued. I pleaded with the gnome not to kill me and was glad when the noise finally tapered off. For the remainder of night, I hid under the covers. I didn't move or breathe. Once the sun came up, I worked up enough courage to approach my desk. My cell phone was lying next to the gnome on "vibrate" mode and the screen read "1 missed call" But just to be sure, I now lock the gnome in my desk drawer whenever I sleep.

SEMESTER 2 LETTER 3

I am tired, worn out, confused, but most importantly, I've finished my first year of university! The last week has been brutal. Days of the week here have no meaning. Ask anybody what day it is, and you will usually hear something along the lines of "two days 'til my next exam."

My friends all have different study habits. One guy parties every night and only begins to study the day before the exam. He apparently takes pills to lower his stress levels; he takes ephedrine to keep his energy up, and he buys Ritalin from a girl on his dorm floor, which he claims cuts study time down to half. Everyone has his or her own ways of coping with exams. Obviously some people cope better than others.

A guy named Howard decided he was sick of physics, or maybe he was just sick of life, so he took a plunge from his fourth-story dorm window. Unfortunately, or rather, fortunately for Howard, he only broke his legs and was forced to write his exam anyway. Exams are very stressful times and, over the past couple of days, I have spent some time with people who are stressed enough to take a "Howardly" leap. I'm not one who handles stress like a champion, but I'm still far better off than many others. During my Chemistry exam, I thought, *Shit! This exam is a killer.* At that exact moment the girl sitting next to me broke down crying. I looked at her and thought, *at least I'm doing better than she is!*

Now that exams are over, I'm sitting in my half-packed residence room enjoying my last couple of hours in the Zoo. It feels like the last day of summer camp. In fact, university is very much like sleep away camp; but instead of being forced to do swim instruction or drama, we are forced to take Molecular Cell Biology and Biochemistry. I must admit that, as at camp, the friendships I have forged here will last forever, and best of all, we get to come back next year and do it all again!

Only next year, I won't be living in a colossus dormitory with thousands of other students. I will be living in an apartment building off-campus with my buddy Mitch. Mitch and I have managed to rent a very cool pad downtown. I will no longer need to share a bathroom with thirty other people, because our apartment has two bathrooms, one for each of us. Upon signing the lease we also learned that our building has a gym, sauna, and hot tub, which is certainly an added bonus.

SUMMER BREAK EDITION

My summer break has been pretty lame! While many of you are out traveling the world, I decided to take two consecutive organic chemistry classes at McGill University back home in Montreal. I have just finished tackling the Organic Chemistry 2 monster, which makes its prerequisite seem like a walk in the park. My sanity is diminishing. The content of the summer course, not to mention the chemicals, have caused me to go mad.

DELTA G (SPONTANEITY)

My dad was giving me a lift to summer school one morning when he purposefully drove his nice, clean, fancy car right through a huge dirty puddle.

"What did you do that for?" I asked.

"I try to do at least one spontaneous thing a day…and that was my spontaneous action for today," he explained.

"I like spontaneity…but that was just stupid! What good came from doing that?" I asked.

"I broke out of my 'comfort zone!' It was fun. Sometimes you have to just do things on impulse without contemplating it forever. Seize the moment before it passes you by. Spontaneity is about taking a chance... doing something you would normally not do and simply hoping for the best."

Well, I took Dad's advice, and it actually worked to my advantage. In my Organic Chemistry 1 class, at the beginning of the summer, I had met a girl named Katie, who had beautiful blue eyes and blonde hair. During the first organic class, she had not said more than a couple of words to me. I got a bad vibe...I figured she thought I was loud and obnoxious (which was probably the truth).

Later, I overheard Katie speaking of putting together a study group, which she did by flirting with the smartest boys in the class. I figured I had been struggling with the material long enough, so I decided to ask Katie if I could join her study group.

I waited for the opportune moment to ask—when she couldn't refuse. It was during lab on a Friday afternoon as she was confirming with each of the group members that they would be at the study session she had planned for Sunday. I walked up to her and told her, in the most platonic way I could, that I wanted in on her study session.

She took my notebook out of my hand and wrote her name and number on the front cover.

"Call me to get my address later on this weekend," she instructed.

I had decided to make it a study weekend. I would study hard Friday night and Saturday, so that I would hopefully be caught up enough to make the review session on Sunday beneficial and impress her with my knowledge.

I walked into my house that evening to find two tickets to the "Just for Laughs Comedy Festival." Everyone in my family was headed to the cottage for the weekend, so if I wanted the tickets, they were mine.

"Thanks, Dad, but this has to be a big study weekend. I can't go tonight," I apologized.

I pulled out my textbook and notebook and began to study. As I reviewed the Grignard reaction my attention was quickly diverted to Katie's name on the front of my notebook.

Maybe it was the way she dotted her "i," or maybe it was her deep blue eyes, or the fact that she didn't seem to like me...I had to speak to her!

Like a reckless man plowing his fancy car through a giant puddle, I picked up the phone and dialed her number.

Unfortunately I got her answering machine.

"Hi Katie, it's Mike from Orgo. I have two tickets to the comedy festival tonight and I was wondering if you wanted to go with me. I know you're probably planning on studying, but I figure a little comedy might do us good. I would feel less guilty going if a fellow classmate was sitting beside me. Who knows…maybe we'll learn by diffusion…?"

I hung up the phone and felt mortified. What had I just done? Who uses words like "diffusion" outside of a lab report? Would she think that I joined the study group simply to get her number? There was no way she was going to call me back.

I spent the next half hour staring at the phone wishing there was some way I could take back my bumbling message. I eventually resorted to studying. Then, the inexplicable happened. The phone rang. It was Katie, and she sounded really excited to join me at the show. I was ecstatic!

I figured it would be an early night, because we both had to study the next day. As we left the show, I thanked her for joining me and asked her if she wanted to stop for a drink.

"You had better believe we are going out for drinks," she said. "It's Friday night!"

This girl was smart, good looking, and definitely knew how to party. After a couple of drinks on Crescent Street in downtown Montreal, I parked my car at her apartment, and we headed to a random loft party in the Old Port.

As we set out onto the dance floor, she asked me if I wanted a piece of gum.

Do I have bad breath? I wondered.

She pulled out her pack but there was only one piece left. She popped it into my mouth.

I must really have bad breath if she's willing to give me her last piece, I thought.

"You didn't want any?" I asked her.

"I figured we could share," she answered, as she leaned in toward me and kissed the gum out of my mouth.

BLAST OFF! From now on I'm driving through every puddle I see!

I did much better in Organic Chemistry 2, and I owe it all to Katie. From that moment on, I began to spend a lot of time "studying" at her apartment. Finally, a crush on a girl had translated into improved marks at school.

Now summer class is finished and Katie is home in Boston. There wasn't enough time for anything significant to solidify between us, but I will always remember the time I spent studying for Organic, even if I don't remember any of the chemistry.

THE GUM INCIDENT

My friends soon noticed that I had been a little down since the end of summer school and they figured it had something to do with the departure of my alleged study partner. They insisted that I head out for a night on the town with them.

Adam, Jake, his girlfriend, and I headed out to a dance club for a night of partying. It was one of those occasions when, instead of grabbing my faded jeans from the first rack in the closet, I reached a little deeper and pulled out my suit.

For me, there is something very ritualistic about putting on a suit. As I unzip the bag and take out my pants, I try to tune in to what I may be thinking at the end of the night, when I have to fold them back up. I hardly envisioned myself having as much fun as I did...

We arrived at the club at about 11:00 p.m. and headed directly to one of the many outside bars. We were acting like big shots, buying rounds for each other, smoking cigars, becoming chummy with the bartenders. We had just about every sugar-saturated shot you can imagine—Amaretto, Liquid Cocaine, B52. We even invented a couple of our own.

It didn't take long for us to become completely inebriated. Jake and his girlfriend hit the dance floor, leaving Adam and me on the prowl. We picked up a couple of beers before we began our female safari. Guys love to hold beer when scoping out women; it is a natural defense mechanism. If you start talking to a woman and she walks away...well, at least you're still clenching a beer.

We made our way toward a couple of good-looking girls and sat down nearby so we could observe them. In our collective alcoholic stupor, we plotted how best to woo them.

I was intrigued by the small brunette, and Adam wanted the tall blonde. They knew they were being pursued. They got up and walked toward the dance floor. We followed...by 12:05 a.m., we had introduced ourselves. By 12:07, we had already broken off into two separate conversations. I happened to end up talking to the tall blonde, and Adam talked to the small brunette. By 12:15, we had our arms around the girls we had been speaking to and we were *dancing*.

I was drunk. I was saying the stupidest things...but she seemed to like it. I remember saying things like, "From far, your bag looks like a cat," and, "You might not be able to tell by looking at me, but I can run really fast." I obviously told her she was the most beautiful girl in the whole club, which might have actually been the truth. There was no swapping of partners after using a line like that.

I figured since we were dancing close, I had best put a piece of gum in my mouth...

The girl was substantially taller than I am. She happened to turn around suddenly to do some grind move with her butt. As she swung her head around, my gum somehow got lodged deep in her hair.

There I was with a hot girl, and I had already managed to get my gum stuck in her hair! *This could ruin everything,* I thought. I continued to dance so that she would not realize that anything was wrong. I took my hands off her hips and tried to pull the gum out of her hair without her noticing. Adam had noticed the dilemma and tried to keep his girl from looking in my direction.

I kept pecking at the glob of gum with my fingers, but I knew that I would have to use force. Adam motioned to me that I should just rip it out. (God forbid I ruin what he had going on with the little brunette he stole away from me.) I grabbed the piece of gum and gave it a good yank. It came out with a few strands of hair and I tossed it across the dance floor.

"Ouch, what the fuck!" she yelled as she spun around to face me.

"I'm sorry. Your hair must have gotten stuck on my watch." I took off my watch and put it into my pocket and promised her that it would not happen again. *Phew*...good recovery. I told her I would make it up to her by buying her a drink.

We ended up having a really awesome time together. She was noticeably upset when I told her that there wouldn't be any subsequent dates, since I was returning to Eastern for another semester the following day.

SEMESTER 3 LETTER 1

I am finally back at Eastern for my second year of college. I now live off-campus in the downtown area, in a beautiful apartment with my roommate Mitch. Our apartment is clean and spacious, and as visitors like to say, "fully hooked up." We have our own washer/dryer, dishwasher, and central air, not to mention a party hall, gym, hot tub, and sauna. We also each have our own private bathroom, which is proving to be essential, since Mitch's already smells like animal.

My room is nice and big. I have a huge L-shaped desk, which took me a full four days to build, and my bed is certainly big enough for two, if not three on the rare occasion. We are on the fourth floor of the building and my window looks out over Richmond, the city's main street. The window is huge, and the blinds don't close, so I can almost always see the downtown action. The other day, I rushed out of the shower, dropped my towel, and began to get dressed, when I heard a small ruckus coming from the terrace below. I guess "seeing the action" through my window is also possible for people on the outside.

THE MYSTERY ROAD TRIP

It's "rush" time again for our fraternity, and now I'm on the initiated side. Most of our events have been alcohol-free, because we want to get to know the new guys that are rushing. Friday night, we had our first alcoholic event. It was called the "Mystery Road Trip." A school bus pulled up to the fraternity house and hundreds of bottles of beer were loaded aboard. All the brothers and rushes boarded the bus and embarked on a journey to an undisclosed location. Nobody, except for the social coordinator, the bus driver, and several alumni knew where we were headed.

After about an hour on the highway, the bus came to an abrupt halt, and we formed the longest piss line Highway 401 has ever experienced. By then, we had speculated that we were headed toward a town called Hamilton. As we approached Hamilton, one of our rushes had the sudden urge to puke; luckily, he managed to get the window open in time. Given the velocity of the bus and the projectile angle of the vomit, all of it splattered on the outside of the bus windows. In fact, it formed interesting streaks and designs along the windows, which everyone marveled at in their drunken stupors.

As we drove into Hamilton, there was an increasing need to pee again. Soon, the emergency exit in the back of the bus was opened and people were attempting the "in-transit pee." Several of the guys had stage fright; that's when the garbage bag emerged. Suddenly, people were peeing into a giant garbage bag in the middle of the bus. I was in tears when the bag was chucked out the window as our visiting gift to Hamilton.

By the time we pulled up to the club, we were all inebriated. People were staring at our big yellow bus splattered with vomit and drenched with piss, containing several dozen rowdy fraternity guys just dying to bust out and make a mess. We arrived at a club where some ten alumni were waiting outside with trays of shots. We might not have a reputation for being the most sophisticated fraternity at Eastern, but we certainly know how to have the most fun.

SEMESTER 3 LETTER 2

THE FILIPINO CLUB

Rush is still going strong. At a recent party our fraternity social coordinator ordered a huge two-foot by four-foot block of ice. He then spent a few hours hollowing a passage through the ice so that drinks could be poured in at one end and come out chilled at the other.

We quickly discovered that the tunnel could be used as a quick and effective way of guzzling beer. We took turns putting our mouths around the hole and chugging copious volumes of beer, as it was poured into the other side.

The next morning, I scrambled to get up in time and nearly missed my bus to campus. As I sat on the bus, I noticed my vision was blurry and my senses were dulled. I slurred out a couple of words to the bus driver then realized..."*SHIT, I'm still drunk.*"

Luckily I only had one short class. I spent the rest of the morning perusing through the University Community Center where Clubs Week was in full effect. Each club was given a booth to showcase its cause and recruit new members. In my inebriated state, I decided to join every club that would accept me.

By lunch I sobered up—but not before I had the chance to join twenty-two clubs including the university Filipino Association.

At first, the Filipino Association president was a little confused as to why I wanted to join.

"Are you sure you want to join? Clearly you're not Filipino, and all our meetings and social events are carried out in Tagalog, our country's native language. You won't even understand what is going on. Do you even know anything about the Philippines?"

I was extremely offended and of course still a little drunk.

I stared him right in the eyes and said, "How dare you question my knowledge of the homeland."

I clicked my heels together, straightened my back and brought my hand above my eye to a salute position.

"*Bei Young Magili, Pershchen sei le Mei Young, I lub Nampousoo... Salei Bohi Boohei...*" I began to sing the Filipino national anthem. As a child I had a Filipino nanny who used to sing me the anthem to help me fall asleep. The club president was stupefied. He instantly apologized and offered me full membership to his club. He handed me a schedule of all the upcoming club events and made me promise that I would attend the upcoming "Chicken Adobo night."

That's how I became a member of the Filipino Association. Who knows...maybe these sorts of memberships will come in handy if I decide to run for some particular political position, or start a secret society.

SEMESTER 3 LETTER 3

THE BUMBLE BEE ATTACK

I was walking across campus the other day when a tall Asian fellow rode by me on a bicycle. As he cycled by, something in his hair caught my eye. Smack down in the middle of his mushroom cut was the largest, fiercest, yellow-striped bumble bee I have ever seen. My eyes remained fixed on it as I contemplated a course of action. But before I knew it, I missed my chance to warn him, and he had passed me by.

It just so happened that this incident occurred during "the days of repentance" of the Jewish New Year. According to Jewish laws, the days between "Rosh Hashanah" (Jewish New Year) and Yom Kippur (Judgment Day) are used to repent all one's transgressions. It is an opportunity to redeem yourself and prove to God that you are worthy of living another year.

I thought about yelling out to the guy on the bike, but people would think I was crazy. I mumbled to myself, "Sucks for him," and turned to walk the other way. Then I heard a prophetic inner voice echo inside my head: *"You have a responsibility...You must warn him...Go!"*

I turned on my heels, looked up at the sky (as if to say, "This better get me into the *Book of Life*,") and then started running. By that time, he was a good fifty feet away from me. I ran after him yelling:

"BUMBLE BEE, BUMBLE BEE, HEAD!"

It was a busy street, and my yelling seemed to have attracted the attention of everyone on the block, including Mr. Mushroom Cut. Still biking, he turned his head to see what the commotion was. To his bewilderment, he saw me chasing after him. Maybe the sound "bumble bee" translates into something threatening in Chinese. Or maybe it was the realization that he was being chased by a short, stocky guy with flailing arms and a huge bobbing knapsack roaring "BUMBLE BEE...HEAD." Whatever the reason, he was scared, and not because he understood that there was a bumble bee on his head.

Naturally, he began to peddle faster and faster, so I ran faster. As I quickened my stride, my sentences grew less and less coherent. "Stop! Or it will get you through your brain." (In hindsight it was probably not the best thing to yell at someone when you are trying to get him to stop.) At this point, the pursuit had become a major focus of attention. Everyone was watching, wondering what the hell was going on.

The gap between us grew too wide. He was too far ahead and moving too fast for me to catch up. I stopped dead in my tracks and let out one final discombobulated yelp, which sounded more like a Harry Potter spell than anything else. People stared at me as if I was some sort of mental-case. I raised both hands up to the sky as if to as God, "Do I at least get credit for trying?" Suddenly, Mushroom Cut was stung on the head. The guy grabbed his head with both hands, letting go of the handlebars. He was subsequently flung like a rag doll off his bike onto a patch of grass.

The funny thing about bees is that they make people act all crazy. Have you ever noticed how, when a bee swoops down next to you, the natural instinct is to jump around thrashing your arms and bobbing your head, as if you are some sort of porpoise? Perfectly justifiable behavior...as long as the people around you can also see the bee. Keep in mind, people standing far away never seem to see the bee; all they see is some crazy person prancing in circles, convulsing through the air.

The insect continued to attack Mr. Mushroom Cut. He immediately jumped back up onto his feet and sent his arms and legs reverberating through the air. He was thrashing about like a fish out of water. The people on the street were in shock. From their perspective this guy was biking away from a pursuer when suddenly some invisible force knocked him off his bike and caused him to turn psycho.

All this happened within seconds of my gibberish chant, while my hands were still shrugged up toward the sky. By the looks of it, I was Eastern's version of Harry Potter. I quickly noticed that all eyes were on me; everyone's face plastered with confusion, afraid to move, afraid they might be doomed to the same fate.

I ran toward Mr. Mushroom Cut, who by this point had escaped the bee and was nursing his new wound. Luckily (apart from the sting) he was totally fine and realized why I had been chasing him.

The whole thing would have never happened if he had been wearing a helmet. As I left the enchanted scene, a pale woman dressed like a Goth with two studs through her nose caught up to me and asked me if I could teach her my magic. I just whispered, "Happy *Rosh Hashanah*," and ran away.

BORISSIO BREW

I have decided to finally put years of chemistry education to use and "synthesize" something of value. Mitch and I have set up a microbrewery in the storage room in our apartment. I have done hours of research and can proudly say that I now have a firm understanding of the beer-brewing process. We are presently on day ten of my mapped out twenty-one-day brewing schedule.

Mitch and I bought all the instruments and apparatus needed to assemble a microbrewery, mainly a bunch of tubes, pails, a glass carboy, and a triple-scale hydrometer. We then had to buy all the ingredients for the beer—pre-caned hops, sugar, and of course, *yeast*. We mixed all the ingredients together, boiled them and then placed them into a primary fermenter. The hardest part about brewing beer is ensuring that everything is completely sterile. Mitch (who is by no means a science student) was totally perplexed as to why I washed everything thoroughly with sodium-bisulfate. I tried to educate him about bacteria and microbes, but to no avail.

Once the "wart" (all the ingredients) was mixed, I "pitched" the yeast. That was about the last time our apartment didn't smell like a brewery. After six days of fermentation, we siphoned the "beer" and "decanted" it into the "secondary glass carboy" fermenter. As it stands, we have less than two days remaining of the secondary fermentation before we "rack" the beer. We should have at least fifty half-liter bottles ready to drink by next week. I have engineered the alcoholic content to be up around 8 percent, but in all likelihood, it will be higher. In theory, each bottle we brew will cost us a maximum of thirty cents in raw material, so we will technically save a tremendous amount of money on booze. We have decided to call our beer "Borissio Brew" in honor of my beloved and infamous stuffed animal Mr. Borissio Elephantine, who has joined me at college as our apartment mascot.

BUS RIDE STORY TIME

Every bus ride has a set of individuals who like to talk loud enough for the whole bus to hear. I must admit, I tend to get quite drawn into these conversations. I might not be looking their way, but I sure am listening. It's human nature; virtually everyone sitting in the bus is covertly listening; otherwise they would be chatting as well. Obviously, the person telling the story wants everyone to overhear what he or she is saying, otherwise the person wouldn't be projecting it to the entire bus. So, in effect, the bus ride becomes story time, and the floor is usually given over to the most animated passenger or the person with the most interesting story. I must admit, I too have been guilty of projecting stories in the bus.

Recently, I was riding the bus with a friend, and I guess without realizing it, we soon became "the storytellers." It was a fairly mundane conversation but I realized that everyone around us was tuned in. Unfortunately, all my friend really wanted to talk about were her wisdom teeth, or lack thereof. She apparently had her wisdom teeth extracted two weeks prior to the conversation and had lots to say. I sat there for a solid ten minutes nodding, as she showed me her gum holes, and I listened patiently to her babble about how massive the extracted teeth were. I couldn't get a single word in edgewise.

Then, suddenly, I remembered that through a weird series of events, I happened to have one of my own wisdom teeth in my backpack. After my wisdom teeth were extracted a few years ago, I had glued them into my stuffed animal Borissio's mouth. Borissio is fairly odd looking elephant head made even more awkward by the half-dozen real human teeth I have collected and affixed into his mouth.

Several months earlier, one of the wisdom teeth had become dislodged from Borissio's mouth. I placed the tooth safely into the hidden pocket in my backpack to be reinserted at a later time. I had forgotten about the tooth's safekeeping until that precise moment on the bus.

Without even thinking of the potential impact, I reached down into the hidden pocket and produced a giant, gangly wisdom tooth. I held the tooth out before my friend's face. "Well, as you can see, my wisdom tooth is actually quite large too." There was a look of terror on her face...and on all the other bus passengers' faces too. "Holy shit, why the hell do you have that with you?" she screamed. I heard several other "Oh my Gods," "Holy shits," and "What a sicko," echo through the bus—proof that people were covertly listening.

I quickly realized how weird I must have seemed to the people around me. Honestly, who carries their extracted wisdom teeth in their school bag? At that point, all eyes were on me. In an attempt to dispel any preconceptions regarding my sanity, I tried to explain myself.

"I *randomly* have this wisdom tooth because, after they were extracted, I inserted them into Borissio's mouth—"

"Sicko," one of the passengers muttered.

"No! Borissio is not a person...It's my stuffed animal elephant," I rebutted. I quickly realized that I was not helping my cause. People were blatantly staring at me, as if I was some awful, demented, tooth fairy wannabe. Truth be told, Borissio is an extremely odd entity, and his presence continues to creep out even those people who are closest to me, let alone strangers.

So what did I do? What I always do when people around me think I'm crazy. I *went with it*. Some situations just can't be recovered from. I threw my head back and my arms in the air and let out an offshoot of the famous Jerry Maguire phrase: "I'm not going to do what you all think I'm going to do. I'm not just going to YANK my teeth out." A large number of passengers disembarked at the next stop...I wonder why?

GROCERY STORE ANTICS

We always seem to get wild when we go to the grocery store. We usually go on Thursday nights in Mitch's fancy Lexus. We strut into the store like two sophisticated college students discussing the menu for an upcoming dinner party we'll be hosting.

Within a matter of seconds, we're playing hide and go seek in the aisles and acting like infants. Mitch usually hijacks the carriage and disappears. I end up having to walk around filling my shirt with all the goods I want. Once my shirt is overflowing with food, he is never anywhere to be found.

One night I was furious that he ran off, so I decided to have the cashier page him on the loud speaker. I pretended to be really distraught. I told the cashier, "I lost my little brother and I cannot find him anywhere. Please help!" The cashier told me she had a five-year-old son who did the same thing whenever they went shopping, so she was very sympathetic to my request.

She was more than happy to call Mitch's name repeatedly on the P.A system, until he came to find me at the front of the store. The cashier was slightly confused when Mitch, a college student, showed up, as opposed to Mitch the toddler she was expecting. I explained to her that we were just toddlers trapped in men's bodies.

The meat section is always good for a couple of laughs. As we were picking our cuts of meat, I noticed an unusually long package. I picked it up and, to my horror, it was the hollowed out carcass of a bunny rabbit. It still had its ears and tail. Mitch wasn't paying attention, so naturally, I slipped the bunny carcass into the cart. Once again, Mitch took control of the cart and began to push it down the cereal aisle. About half way down the aisle, I heard a horrifying shriek. Mitch had met Thumper. I figured I'm new to the whole cooking thing; I'm not ready to cook something as complex as rabbit just yet, so I bought Thumper for entertainment purposes. I can just imagine the look on a guest's face when they reach into the freezer for some vodka and find a frozen rabbit carcass.

Getting our groceries up to the apartment is the most stressful part of the shopping experience. Mitch usually pulls his car up to the front doors and we quickly carry all of our parcels through the lobby and into the mezzanine. Then Mitch helps me load the elevator with all the parcels and leaves to move his car. My job is to ride the elevator to our floor and unload all our parcels into our apartment.

I was working feverishly to unload all thirty parcels out of the elevator when, all of a sudden, the elevator door shuts with me on the outside. *SHIT!* Before I knew it, the groceries were going on a solo ride up sixteen flights. It was as if someone were pressing buttons on the inside of the elevator. I ran up and down dozens of flights of stairs trying to "catch" my groceries.

"Excuse me, Sir, have you seen an elevator full of groceries go by?" I asked a neighbor. I finally caught up with the groceries on the seventh floor, and to my surprise, everything was just as I had left it—except for Thumper. He had somehow managed to fall out of his bag. And I can only imagine that, to this day, he haunts the building, riding up and down the elevator.

THE LAB GUINEA PIG

My physiology labs is all about conducting research experiments. Most of the labs involve animals, but a fair portion of the lab involves using classmates as test subjects.

I was chosen as the group guinea pig in our last lab. My lab partners hooked me up to electrodes. The objective was to stimulate a "measurable" twitch down my forearm and into my middle finger. My arm was placed in a restraint and each lab partner was assigned different tasks. One guy was monitoring the data readings, the dumb guy in the group was in charge of regulating the current and ensuring everything was hooked up properly, and the group female was in charge of delivering the stimulus—an *electric* stimulus.

A normal human arm should start to twitch anywhere between fifteen to thirty volts. I was cranked up to forty and felt nothing. So we cranked it to seventy, and still I felt nothing. We cranked it up to 100 volts and still no response. Then the idiot in charge of the hook-up realized that a wire was unplugged on the stimulator. He plugged it in without turning down the voltage, and I received the most God-awful shock of my life. Every muscle in my body clenched up; my hand developed a mind of its own and flew up into the air. My first impulse was to grab the stimulus, which was a big mistake. By grabbing the stimulus, I created a current through both my arms and into my chest. I stood there convulsing for a couple of seconds, until one of my lab partners knocked the stimulus out of my hand.

I then resigned my position as lab rat and realized my hair had become even bushier and more squirrel-like. I vowed that next time the group idiot would be the lab rat, and we would see how he liked the volts. The T.A. said if I had endured any higher voltage, I would have, without a question, shat my pants. I don't think there could be anything more humiliating than soiling oneself in a communal laboratory setting.

THE BEER DISASTER

Finally "Borissio Brew" was ready for consumption. We figured there is no better authority on beer than our fraternity brothers. We invited the guys over to our apartment to watch the game and savor our concoction. Initially the beer was a big hit. It tasted no worse than any other cheap draft beer.

Soon people were drinking seconds and thirds. The beer seemed to impart a good buzz. However, once the beer had time to seep deep into the intestines it began to wreck havoc. Personally, my guts began to gurgle followed by excruciating abdominal cramps. Others experienced a sudden onset of diarrhea. Everyone seemed to be affected by flatulence.

Apparently explosive farts are a known side effect of home-brewed beer. The combination of indigestible complex carbohydrates coupled with large amounts of yeast begets gas and osmotic diarrhea.

Soon our guests were trying to out-fart one another, and attempts were made to light the farts on fire, as well as capture them in jars. At anyone else's house I would have thought the scenario was hilarious. I just didn't enjoy it going on in my own living room over carpeted floors. A large line for the bathroom formed. One after another my fraternity brothers desecrated my pristine toilet. I tried to encourage the party to relocate to the fraternity house; after all, there were multiple toilets there, but everyone seemed to be enjoying the relative cleanliness of ours.

By the time I used the toilet there was *solid* proof that others had been there first. I was forced to use the "octagon technique" in my own private bathroom. I vowed never to brew my own beer, or host a fraternity get-together at my home, ever again.

***** **THE EASTERN SECRET SOCIETY** *****

Dear Eastern Student,

My name is Borissio Elephantine, but who I am is of little importance. I have been handed over the position of leader of the Eastern Secret Society. Though I have every intention of keeping the society as clandestine as it has been for the past few decades, I do however desire to flex our orchestrating ability.

A new global phenomenon has tweaked our attention, and we would like to bring it home to Eastern. This social phenomenon, known as the "flash mob," which began in New York and relies on e-mail, appears to be spreading worldwide. Flash mobbing, in case you aren't on top of the latest fad, is the sudden but orchestrated appearance of a crowd in a public place. The crowd acts out a loosely defined, often bizarre, set of actions and then abruptly disappears. These crowds are always peaceful; they have no social or political agenda, and their *raison d'être* is simply to engage in spontaneity and have a little fun. These events are a blast for the participants and nothing short of a confusing spectacle for people experiencing it on the periphery.

I want to initiate one of these flash mobs right here on our Eastern campus. Obviously, this gathering will be peaceful and solely for entertainment. Imagine, suddenly at some preset time, a large crowd materializing somewhere on campus, pointing up at the sky and then suddenly bursting into applause (for example), then dissipating minutes later. Imagine an event that would conjure up some questions, give the newspaper staff something interesting to write about and maybe raise a little spirit. Should this "flash mob" be successful, maybe it can eventually be coupled with some form of charity or beneficial cause.

If you like this idea and want to be informed of future organized flash mobs, please reply to this e-mail. Forward this e-mail to all friends whom you feel would be partial to participating in this sort of event. The goal is to add as many keen Eastern students to the mailing list as possible. If you are a member of a varsity team, fraternity/sorority, or club please pass the message along.

The success of this idea lies in the effective dispersal of and response to this e-mail.

Best of luck,

Borissio Elephantine

Leader of the Eastern Secret Society

SEMESTER 3 LETTER 4

The last month has been quite hectic. I have taken exam after exam and written paper after paper. I have set an interesting sociological phenomenon into motion, and I have been actively involved in fraternity affairs. I figure my life is fairly similar to that of most other college students. However, I seem to have a predisposition for ending up in bizarre or comical situations while going about my normal daily routine.

GORDON THE GECKO

It was a beautiful, clear night just prior to the onset of mid-term exams. The fraternity house was clean and decked out, ready for the night's party. I was supervising the setup crew when one of the pledges brought an anomaly in the basement to my attention. The basement of our fraternity house is one step below "dungeon"...you can literally find bones down there if you look hard enough. Legend has it that a fire-breathing dragon once dwelled in the darkest pits of the fraternity's basement. Brothers who live in the house still claim to hear monster noises coming from the basement during the wee hours of the morning.

"Mike, I don't mean to bother you, but there is some sort of lizard hanging out in the basement," the pledge said. Confused, I made my way downstairs only to find a small, living, breathing gecko hanging out between a bag of old hockey gear and a pile of political science textbooks from the 1970s.

Strange, I thought. The gecko looked old. It had a huge stump where I guess its tail had once been, probably a war scar from battling with whatever other scary creatures lived down here. I immediately named the creature Gordon, and I ran up to the fraternity library to gather some information about my new friend.

It turned out Gordon is of the family *Gekkonidae*, a vocal, nocturnal lizard, only found in warm climates. Imagine how relieved the guys were to learn that the scary noises that had them shaking in their beds was just a little gecko roaring in the basement, amplified through the heating vents. It turns out some fraternity brother five years ago had Gordon as a pet. Unfortunately, or fortunately for Gordon, he escaped and had found refuge in the fraternity house basement, where he has lived ever since.

I was downright impressed by Gordon and his awesome survival. Later that evening, when the party started and some seventy sorority girls swarmed the house, I started giving guided tours of Gordon for all ladies brave enough to enter the dungeon to see him. I don't know if it was my enthusiasm or the free-flowing alcohol, but several ladies in formal attire opted to follow me down into the dungeon. Unfortunately, Gordon's survival skills had kicked in and he was nowhere to be seen, so I eventually called off the tours.

At a later time, after I had consumed a fair amount of alcohol myself, one of the ladies (who had been on an earlier tour) asked me if I would be willing to take her back down on a second attempt to meet Gordon. Obviously, I obliged…but once again he was nowhere to be seen. However, the nice young lady refused to go back upstairs until she got to see a gecko. I doubled my efforts to find Gordon, but she suddenly grabbed me by the crotch of my pants and said, "Gordon is not the only type of lizard I want to see!"

FRATERNITY HALLOWEEN PARTY

Before you start passing judgment on fraternities, I would just like to state that it is not all about partying and girls (though that is a major part). Our chapter held a food drive several weekends ago. We went all around Ithaca collecting non-perishable food items for our city's hungry. Every member of the fraternity worked hard and we managed to bring in 9,995 pounds of food. About the equivalent weight of an adolescent male elephant.

On the night of the food drive, we threw a Halloween party at our fraternity house to thank everyone who had volunteered. Mitch and I were both zonked from collecting food all day, and we neglected to prepare costumes. Ten minutes before we were suppose to head over to the fraternity house, we decided to go as twins. And by that I don't mean we dressed the same...quite the contrary.

We decided we would show up at the fraternity house wearing nothing but diapers. We would be toddler twins, but where might one buy adult diapers at 10:30 p.m. on a Saturday night? We dropped in to a local twenty-four-hour supermarket, and to our astonishment a package of diapers cost over twenty bucks...a price we were not willing to pay. Since we only needed two diapers, Mitch had a plan. He brought an open package of diapers to the cash register (which he had ripped open himself) and we began to engage in negotiations with the cashier.

"Can you make us a deal on an open package of diapers?" Mitch asked. While negotiations were ongoing, a classmate of mine happened to walk by and was quite confused to find me trying to bargain down the price of a package of Depends. She scampered over, almost over-excited to tell me something. She pulled me aside and boasted that she had received some sort of correspondence from the "Eastern Secret Society."

She explained that the Society was so secretive that barely anybody knew of its existence. The leader of the Society, "BORISSIO ELEPHANTINE," was never seen or heard, yet was somehow omnipresent.

I asked her why she was telling me this. She said, "You're just the type of person who would appreciate this kind of thing," and then she went on to tell me that the society was organizing a FLASH MOB. Naturally this news intrigued me...

Eventually, Mitch managed to broker a deal with a newbie cashier. He sold us two diapers for a mere two dollars. We arrived at the fraternity house fashionably late, and virtually naked. It might just have been my boldest entrance ever. As we walked in, people stood up, a passage formed, and all eyes were fixed on us. The whole experience was actually quite liberating, literally. Once you're standing in front of a girl with only a small piece of cotton covering your package, introducing yourself is the easy part.

***** THE EASTERN SECRET SOCIETY *****

Dear flash mob members,

I first want to thank you and officially welcome you as members of the EASTERN FLASH MOB. As of yesterday, we hit "critical mass" and I am now confident to issue a set of directives for our first mob.

I would just like to quickly reiterate that a flash mob is a peaceful gathering. We are not protesting, nor are we lobbying for any specific cause. We are simply a group of individuals who are gathering in one place to carry out a loosely defined set of actions, as we are entitled by our country's Bill of Rights. I have reviewed the university's Constitution and there is nothing that prohibits us from engaging in a flash mob, as long as we abide by the university's rules and regulations. In no way will this flash mob defile university property or put anyone in danger. IF YOU WILL NOT ABIDE BY THE UNIVERSITY'S REGULATIONS PLEASE DO NOT PARTICIPATE IN THE FLASH MOB. Everyone participating in the mob must take responsibility for his/her actions. Neither FLASH MOB EASTERN nor the Eastern Secret Society will be held responsible for what each student individually does beyond the instructions that have been issued.

Our first flash mob will occur on Wednesday, November 19. The mob will begin at precisely 12:54 p.m. and will end by 12:58 p.m. It takes place between classes, so everyone should be able to attend.

The mob will converge on Concrete Beach on the left side of the new purple awning. I would like everyone to wear at least one visible piece of red clothing, which will help mobbers identify one another. Timing is crucial: everyone must be on time! Please synchronize your watches to the time according to the Government of the United States website.

The mob will transpire as follows:

Everyone should try to be in the general Concrete Beach area by 12:53. If you are early, just hang around on the sidelines. THIS MOB WILL TAKE PLACE RAIN OR SHINE! To be safe, I suggest everyone brings an UMBRELLA; it might even contribute to the aesthetic effect.

At exactly ten seconds to 12:54, a designated member of the flash mob will be standing in the location where the flash mob will occur. He/she will then drop a plastic cup filled with pennies and that is your cue to SWARM. By 12:54, I want there to be a huge mob where the pennies have been dropped. (You may pick up a penny if you like.)

Once the mob has formed (roughly a couple of seconds after 12:54) I want everyone pointing up toward the sky. You may shield your eyes if you like. Pretend you are looking up at a giant potato heading for Earth. You may comment to the people standing around you about how huge the potato is. Pretend to be confused or frightened, BECAUSE EVENTUALLY THE POTATO WILL HIT THE EARTH.

Get into it. I want the people passing by to stop and look up at the sky. If anyone asks what you are looking at, just describe a giant potato. This phase will last for approximately two minutes.

At 12:56, a designated flash mob member will start to chant, "Mash Potato." Everyone should join in and the chant should get progressively louder. Everyone must chant in unison, "Mash Potato, Mash Potato." You guys can jump around, dance, and be animated during the chanting.

At 12:57, the chanting will stop only to be replaced by a loud applause. People may yell, "Potato Head," randomly if they like.

At 12:58, everyone must flee the scene. Literally the minute your watch reads 12:58, you must split away from the mob. I suspect everyone will want to run to class anyway. It is important that the mob disintegrates as spontaneously as it formed.

A RECAP

12:54 Everyone SWARMS where coins have been dropped.

12:54-12:56 Point up at the sky and speak of an approaching object (potato)

12:56 Chant "Mash Potato"

12:57 Applause. Random bursts of "Potato Head"

12:58 Everyone has vanished!

This is, in effect, a very loosely defined script. I ask you all to follow these instructions, but please add your own bit of character to it. Don't just chant "Mash Potato"; dance at the same time, form a Conga line? Be creative! Most importantly, have fun.

Keep in mind this mob is short (in the order of four minutes). I hope you can all find the time to come out and have a little fun. Once again, this mob will take place even if it is raining. SO BRING AN UMBRELLA.

I hope to see all of you at 12:54 p.m. on Wednesday.

Take care and good luck,

Borissio Elephantine

Leader of the Eastern Secret Society

SEMESTER 3 LETTER 5

BUS PHENOMENA

To get around at school, I rely heavily on the Ithaca Transit bus system. The buses come infrequently and, when they do stop, they are usually filled to the gills. As uncomfortable as riding the bus could be, there is a social element that I have come to enjoy. Aside from Story Time, I have noticed several phenomena that take place on buses, a few of which I will describe for you.

The first Bus Phenomenon I call the "Bowling Lane Phenomenon." This event usually takes place on rainy days when the floor of the bus becomes wet and slippery. Other factors that contribute to this effect are a crowded bus and a mental-case bus driver. Basically what happens is as follows. The bus becomes crammed way beyond a safe capacity. People are so squished that they cannot even extend their arms to hold onto the railings. Then, as the bus driver either accelerates rapidly or brakes suddenly, some weakly balanced individual (in most cases it is a senior citizen) slips, falls, and starts rolling toward the back of the bus like a bowling ball. Similar to the way the bowling ball knocks over pins, this sliding senior citizen knocks over every individual in his or her path. I have unfortunately been knocked over in one of these brutal "strikes." Let me tell you, it is a wonderful way to begin the day.

A second phenomenon I have come to observe is when people miss their stops due to lack of access to the exit, or when either they or their belongings become ensnared aboard. True unintentional episodes of entrapment occur rarely. Recently, I was fortunate enough to witness one. It was really warm aboard the bus. Passengers opened the windows, which slide open horizontally. As one guy slid his window closed, it caught the hair of a woman who was sleeping against the window behind him. When the bus came to the women's stop she jumped to her feet and let out a horrifying yelp, as she almost ripped off her scalp. Frighteningly enough, this woman was tethered to her seat by her own hair. The poor women had already missed her stop before the guy in front of her successfully opened the window and freed her hair.

The worst by far is bringing groceries home on the bus. As I stroll through the grocery store aisles, I forget that I only have two short little arms. My stomach overcomes my mental reasoning, and I end up with the daunting task of having to transport ten grocery bags on the bus. The third bus phenomenon I have experienced I call "The Yard Sale." It occurs when an individual transporting a large load falls or drops a bag, and the items become scattered throughout the bus. In fear of experiencing yet another yard sale, I often opt to go hungry, rather than go shopping. My mother knows of this reality all too well, for usually, whenever I suffer from a pang of hypoglycemia, I call her to complain.

COOKING LESSON

Last week, I was too lazy to transport a load of groceries on the bus. At the lowest point, all I had in the house were three frozen chicken breasts, a can of cranberry sauce, a jar of honey, and a single pickle. In a bout of hunger I decided to make chicken using only these ingredients. It was around 10:30 p.m. when I began the cooking fiasco. I defrosted the chicken, washed it, then placed it on a cookie sheet and smothered it in cranberry sauce and honey. It was not a conventional preparation but I didn't care; I was starving. I placed a call home to Mom at around 11:00 p.m. to complain about how hungry I was and to inquire how long chicken had to bake.

To my dismay, I learned that chicken must bake for at least an hour. That seemed unacceptable. I hadn't eaten all day. I was weak and famished; there was no way I could survive another hour without food. I pleaded with my Mom (as if she governed how fast chicken bakes) for a few minutes until she cut me a deal.

"I'll tell you what, bake the chicken for forty-five minutes then put on the broiler for an additional five minutes and that should cook it. That's the best I can do," she said.

I agreed to those terms. At least that way, I could eat ten minutes sooner. I turned on the oven, slid in my cranberry honey chicken, and set an alarm so I wouldn't waste a single minute until I could eat. Forty-five minutes later, the alarm sounded and I sprinted to the kitchen to turn on the broiler, only I didn't turn on the broiler. In a fit of excitement I accidentally hit the oven cleaner button instead.

My oven went into heavy lockdown. KA-CHING, KA-CHING, KA-CHING: three metal latches slid into place, and the oven immediately became a high-security poultry incinerator. At first I was really confused as to why the oven door locked, but as my chicken began to scorch, I realized what was going on. I pressed every button on the panel, but I could not get the oven door to release. Driven by hunger, I even took a screwdriver and tried to pry open the door, but to no avail.

The delicious smell of honey cranberry chicken filled the apartment air, as anger and delirium filled my mind. I finally dropped to my knees before the oven, peered in through the glass window at the beautifully succulent morsels of chicken now engorged in flames.

It was just at this moment that Mitch walked into the apartment. Imagine how confused he was to find his roommate down on his knees with his nose pressed up against the oven window with tools spread out all over the kitchen floor and the weird smell of burnt cranberry honey chicken in the air.

I eventually conceded that the oven was not opening any time soon. I ate the last remaining pickle and expired for the night. Some six hours later, the oven buzzed for about a minute and the door unlocked. I took the three charred cranberry honey chicken breasts out and tossed them directly into the garbage.

QUANTUM PHYSICS

The following day, still during a period of relative hunger, I came across a fortunate, or rather unfortunate, find. I had finished class for the day and I was waiting at the bus stop when I had the sudden urge to use the washroom. I had just about five minutes until my bus arrived, more than enough time to dash over to the Physics washroom (my favorite bathroom on campus), pee, and still be back before the bus arrived. There was no way of anticipating the mess I was about to get myself into.

As I exited the men's washroom, still on schedule, I happened to pass by the Physics professor's lounge. There before me was a wonderful display of food. There was a beautiful array of muffins, donuts, and fruit, not to mention pyramids of juice cartons and coffee. A starving student's heaven! Naturally, I needed to take a closer look. As I loitered in the doorway, my stomach began to take control of my body. Before I knew it, I was standing over the tray of muffins with my arm outstretched, ready to pluck a beautifully plump chocolate muffin. A short internal battle between the mind and the stomach ensued, but in the end, I devoured the muffin.

Then suddenly one of the Physics faculty members started talking to me. "Go ahead, help yourself. Eat as much as you like." His tone was very comforting and sympathetic, almost as if he knew that what was to come would be punishment enough for my actions. With this new-found invitation I began to feast.

Just as I began to wonder why the Physics faculty was hosting a free snack time, the lounge door slammed shut. "Excuse me everyone, excuse me…Can everyone please take a seat? We would like to begin…" I quickly jumped up and dashed toward the door, but it was no use, the portal had been shut. I was trapped. Still eating, I had little choice but to take a seat in a comfortable lounge chair sandwiched between two bald Physics professors.

Only at that point did I realize that the lounge was filled with at least a hundred bald men and women, all of whom had PhDs in physics, no doubt. I was one of three individuals below the age of thirty.

The Chairman of the Physics faculty took the floor. "We are honored today, for it is not every day we have the pleasure of hosting a man who is a foremost authority in his field. I take great honor and pleasure in introducing Dr. Yorkibovlovsky, who has come all the way from Cambridge University to share his interpretations on modern revolutions in quantum theory."

OH SHIT...Wasn't that the stuff that ruined my life last year? I thought as I watched my bus leave through the lounge window. Everyone seemed to have taken out a pen and notebook. So, to not seem like some idiot off the street, I reached into my bag and pulled out my own pen and notebook and proceeded to take notes. The first five minutes of the lecture were quite abstract but easy to conceptualize. I actually thought I was experiencing a newfound interest in the subject. The lecturer described how "once two particles interact, they remain entangled as they verge on infinity. So if two particles collide and one remains in the lecture room and the other travels to the moon, what you do to the particle in the lecture room will also have a direct impact on the particle that has traveled to the moon."

Honestly, I was quite intrigued by the theories he was describing, until about the tenth minute when he began to describe a particle's propagation in the fifth dimension. That's when my brain gave me an ultimatum: either tune out or explode. (I had this morbid image of my head blowing up and all my hair splattering onto the heads of the two bald professors sitting next to me). The lecture quickly sky-rocketed above my realm of comprehension. From that point on, all I heard was WOMP, WOMP, WOMP.

Halfway through the lecture, Dr. Quantum Physics decided to crack a joke. I kid you not, this was not a conventional joke; it was a clear-cut physics joke that only a physicist could understand. After explaining some concept, he said in a mocking voice, "...and this is awfully reminiscent of Plank's early theorem." Everyone burst into a fit of laughter. In utter confusion, I too let out a nervous chuckle. Both bald professors sitting to either side of me simultaneously turned to face me and gave me a stern stare, which could only mean, "Shut up UNDERGRADUATE!"

With every passing minute, the lecture became even more intolerable. Eventually, even one of the Physics professors sitting next to me fell asleep and began to drool. At the end of the lecture, the floor opened up for a question period. I had thought of a couple of intelligent questions but I figured it was best I focused my attention on making an escape.

I did eventually end up back outside at my bus stop. Ironically, as I stood there, I realized, *Oh shit I HAVE TO PEE AGAIN,* and as I looked down at my watch, I saw it had been exactly one hour since I first made my way to the Physics building. That was one hour of my life that I will never get back.

THE FLASH MOB

Eastern had its first Flash Mob orchestrated by a newly popularized "Secret Society." Several of my friends who participated were featured on the front page of the Eastern Gazette the next day. Basically, a mob of people dressed in red had converged just outside the University Community Center. They amassed after one person dropped a cup of pennies on the ground. They then pointed up at the sky and pretended that a giant potato was going to hit the earth. After a minute or two they began to chant "Mash Potato," followed by roaring applause and random yelps of "Potato Head." I, along with the rest of the Eastern community, am very intrigued by this scheme, as I enjoyed the spontaneity of it all. The event left the entire campus curious about the potential existence of a secret society on campus, but more importantly, wondering, "Who is Borissio Elephantine?"

SEMESTER 3 LETTER 6

I have now banished myself to the library in preparation for finals, so all the little projects I have been working on have been put on hold. As most of you have already realized, out of my infinite desire to control the world, I created the Eastern Flash Mob as a social experiment and, before I knew it, dozens of students were joining the mailing list. It sort of scared the hell out of me. I never envisioned myself as a cult leader. But, hey, what's not to like about the power to cause a mob to form on campus and pretend potatoes are falling from the sky?

MILK CHALLENGE

Last week was our fall semester fraternity initiation. It's a week of fun, followed by the most grueling sequence of events that renders you an "initiate." I was happy to be on the initiate side this year. During the week leading up to initiation, our pledges took part in many fun activities, some of which were done in tandem with sorority pledges.

During the pre-initiation week, *nobody* was allowed to consume alcohol. None of the events entailed drinking liquor. However, it is customary for the pledge class to go pranking together, so there was a definite need to stockpile vomit. If you need a large quantity of vomit, but you are not allowed to drink alcohol, what can be used to induce reversed peristalsis in its stead? The one and only "Milk Challenge." Everyone willing to participate was given four liters of milk to drink in the allotted time of one hour. Believe me, there was an unimaginable volume of barf collected. I laughed hysterically the entire time; something about grown men fighting over which pail they were going to barf into made me lose it.

I am told that late that evening the pledges hoisted the collected vomit up onto the roof of a sorority house and then carefully funneled it into the fireplace chimney. The prank elicited a rather drastic retaliation. The morning after, everyone awoke to discover that the entire outside of our fraternity house had been decorated with homosexual pornography. Pictures were plastered onto every inch of the house using maple syrup as an adhesive.

These pranking cycles can go on forever. If we retaliated, the cycle would just continue to propagate. I proposed we do something subtle. We should just pick up a couple of dozen mice or crickets and let them in through the sorority mail slot. They didn't have to know we did it, but we could still enjoy the hysteria.

SEMESTER 4 LETTER 1

LUNCH WITH ANNA

My good friend Anna (my neighbor last year in Residence) has the same lunch break as I. We meet every day in the same little corner of the university food court and spend an hour flirtatiously poking fun at each other.

Recently, I happened to get up for a washroom break during lunch, and on the way back to our table, I noticed an unsupervised cordless microphone. Naturally I gravitated toward it. I was just about to pick it up and yell, "Anna's meat sandwich is old and slimy" (as a final blow in the day's round of bickering), but the DJ spotted me reaching for it and yelled, "Pick that up, and I'll cut the power."

"Oh come on, Dude...I just want to say something to my friend Anna sitting down there," I pleaded and pointed.

"What did you want to say to this Anna girl?" he asked.

I gave him a quick synopsis of our daily banter and told him that I wanted to make fun of her meat sandwich.

"I'll tell you what..." he suggested. "I can't let you talk on the microphone because then everyone will want to do it, but why don't you just tell me your name and I will be sure to dedicate the next song to Anna's meat sandwich."

It sounded like a fair offer, so I thanked him and returned to our table. I had a huge smile plastered across my face.

"What are *you* so happy about?" Anna asked.

"Oh nothing…Just wait 'til the song is over. The DJ has a special message for you."

I sat there gleaming. I was excited to see Anna's expression when the DJ made us the center of attention and doled out the final blow in our day's flirtatious banter.

Only that is not what happened at all. At the end of the song, the DJ came onto the microphone and said, "Hey, everyone! I just want to take a moment to dedicate the next song on behalf of a friend of mine… Mike, will you please stand up?" Obviously, I didn't just stand up, I jumped up onto my chair, very animated. All eyes were on me. I loved the attention.

"Everyone say hello to Mike…" ("Hi, Mike," the audience bellowed.) "OK, Mike, where is your friend Anna?" I pointed proudly at little Anna who was blushing with embarrassment. "Well, Anna…Mike has a message he wanted me to announce to you." I was in heaven. This was going to be priceless.

"Mike just wanted me to let you know that he wants to stick his meat between your two little buns."

I quickly dropped down onto my ass. I was mortified. This was not what was supposed to happen. The joke had just done a complete one eighty reversal, and now I was the punch line.

I was as red as a tomato. Anna looked at me and asked, "Did you really ask him to say that?"

"Of course not …" I gasped.

I wanted to die. My moment of infamy was no longer the helium story; hell, only a hundred people saw me screw that up. This was live, primetime; everyone in the University Community Center food court was watching and laughing. The DJ was relentless. "Mike and Anna sitting in a tree K-I-S-S-I-N-G!" We went about eating, and he eventually stopped. Anna, being the sport she is, just laughed it off. In hindsight, I guess I was a little naïve; maybe I had just gotten a shot of my own medicine.

The ordeal only gave Anna more ammunition to tease me with.

"You always try to one-up me, and it always seems to backfire in your face," she laughed.

This time, I truly was humiliated. It would take something huge to come back from this one.

"Who do you think you are?" Anna laughed. "I hope you realize that people are unpredictable. You think you control the world? Obviously, the guy is not going to help you if he could just as easily use your situation to get a laugh...a life lesson for you!" she exclaimed.

She continued to rip into me. "You never seem to realize that things don't always work out as planned. The whole world doesn't revolve around Mike Rubin the Great!"

I was being lectured by a girl who was drinking her hot chocolate with a spoon. The incessant slurping sounds were bothering me more than her lecturing.

"STOP! Just drink the damn hot chocolate from the cup. Stop slurping it from the spoon!" I yelled.

Anna held the spoon up above her head as if it was some sort of weapon that she was about to surrender.

"Mike Rubin, controller of the universe, hereby decrees that thou shall not drink hot chocolate from a spoon," she proclaimed.

"I never said I was controller of the universe—just Eastern," I joked.

Suddenly, the gears in my head began to turn. An amazing idea popped into my head, an idea that would redeem me and put Anna in her place once and for all. I had a plan that would show her just how "controlling" I could be. I packed up my belongings, kissed her on the cheek, and virtually disappeared before she had time to unfreeze from her pose. I ran to the nearest Internet connection to set my plan in motion.

***** **EASTERN SECRET SOCIETY** *****

Hello members,

I just want to congratulate you all on our first mob. For those of you who were not there, I'm sure you all saw the picture on the front page of the Eastern Newspaper. It was a perfect inaugural event. Those who participated were full of energy and certainly left everyone asking, "What the hell just happened?"

The next mob will take place this coming Monday. It will begin at roughly 12:54 p.m., and it will end by 12:57 p.m. It takes place between classes, so everyone should be able to attend.

The mob will take place inside the University Community Center (in the center of the Atrium). I would like everyone to dress in black, which will help mobbers identify one another. As a further means of unification, I invite all participants to bring a silver kitchen spoon to be held in their right hand. Timing is crucial; everyone must be on time!

The mob will transpire as follows:

Everyone should meet in the hallway by the entrance to the bar in the Atrium at exactly 12:54 p.m. We will amass there until precisely 12:55 p.m., at which point one individual will yell "Flash Mob." On that cue, everyone will run to the center of the Atrium and FREEZE! Get creative with your poses; freeze however you like. If you are a shy person just stand perfectly still. No matter how you decide to pose, I ask that you hold your silver spoon in your right hand. Those of you who are really enthusiastic can hold it up high in the air.

When you pick your spot to freeze, please choose it in such a way that you are not totally obstructing traffic or blocking any stairways or exits. It would be ideal if everyone could freeze at one-meter intervals so that people can walk through us instead of around us. (The best example I can give is that I want people passing by to feel like they are in a wax museum.)

At 12:57 p.m., an individual will once again yell, "Flash Mob," and everyone should instantly unfreeze and disperse.

A RECAP

12:54 p.m. Everyone meet wearing black with a spoon in your hand at the front entrance to the bar. (If you forget the spoon it is not the end of the world.)

12:55 p.m. Phase leader will yell, "Flash Mob," and everyone will swarm the Atrium and freeze.

12:55-12:57 p.m. Everyone will remain frozen with a spoon in their right hand. All members who arrive late to the mob just jump in and freeze.

12:57 p.m. The phase leaders will signal to unfreeze and everyone should leave the area in a random fashion.

This mob is very short, so it is vital that everyone arrives on time. Most importantly, have fun participating. The more people who show up, the more effective the mob will be. Even those of you who have class can participate in this mob without being late.

I hope to see you at 12:54 p.m. on Monday.

Take care and good luck,

Borissio Elephantine

Leader of The Eastern Secret Society

SEMESTER 4 LETTER 2

REDEMPTION

Anna and I continued to meet for lunch as usual. The Monday after our embarrassing mishap with the DJ, she once again realized I was up to something.

"Mike, what is going on? You have a smile from ear to ear, and you checked your watch five times in the last three minutes!" she noted.

"I'm a little anxious," I said.

"Anxious about what?" she asked mockingly.

"It's no easy job being leader of the Eastern Secret Society," I said very casually.

Anna just let out a huge laugh. "Here we go again, Mike Rubin and his endless attempt to convince me that he controls the world..."

I checked my watch again and whispered, "Come with me, I'll prove it to you."

"This I've got to see. I thought you already learned your lesson with the whole microphone ordeal. Please don't embarrass me again."

We left the food court and headed for the Atrium in the University Community Center. We stood in the middle of the Atrium, and Anna once again resumed her teasing.

"Wow, Mike...lots going on here," she said sarcastically. "Can we head back and finish our lunch now?"

My watch read exactly 12:55 p.m. I leaned over to Anna and whispered, "Watch this."

I yelled, "FLASH MOB!" and suddenly people dressed in black came running from all directions. Most people were holding a spoon or some variation of a spoon. One guy ran out with a shovel, another with a large candy scooper.

Dozens of mobbers invaded the Atrium and froze in creative positions. It was incredible. Everyone who was not involved was dumbstruck and downright confused, including Anna. Photographers from the Eastern media were snapping pictures and a confused murmur filled the Atrium. At 12:57 p.m. someone yelled, "Unfreeze," and everyone dispersed.

"What the hell just happened? I demand an explanation. How the hell did you do that?" Anna asked.

"I told you, I am the leader of the Eastern Secret Society," and that was all I had to say.

THE SINUSOIDAL PEEP SHOW

I have been doing stationary cycling classes known as "spinning classes" at least twice a week. I'm usually only one of two males in the class, but don't be fooled; these are by no means easy classes. In fact, you control the resistance so you can choose exactly how hard you want to work. Most of the ladies lower their resistance to nearly nothing and just let their legs "spin" at a million RPM so it looks really cool, but there is no actual cardio benefit.

In a recent class of all women, the instructor said, "Well, everybody, today we will be working on our sprints. I want everyone to crank down your resistance."

There is something about sitting on a hard little stationary bike seat and having my legs spin really fast that makes me uneasy. I think it's a gender thing.

"Ok, we will be doing individual sprints today; that means when I point to you, I want you to sprint as hard as you can for fifteen seconds and everyone else will cheer you on," the instructor continued.

I neglected to lower the tension on my stationary bike. I figured she wouldn't point to me anyway.

Given my luck, I was the first one she pointed to. I started to cycle as fast as I could at the current resistance, but she seemed displeased. She jumped off her bike and ran up to me.

"How do you expect to sprint when your resistance is so high!" she yelled, as she reduced the tension on my bike. "NOW SPRINT LIKE YOUR LIFE DEPENDS ON IT!"

My legs moved faster, but there was no way I was going all out. I feared the inevitable, and I hoped she too would realize the terrible outcome that would undoubtedly ensue if my legs moved any faster.

"What's keeping you back?" she yelled. "Everyone encourage him! No one else will get a turn until I see a strong sprint."

Picture me sitting on the bike, everyone around me watching and cheering. Imagine this short little middle-aged cycling instructor (who probably spends two hours a day at a tanning salon with her leathery skin) trying to psych me up by yelling in my face.

Then imagine looking down at my legs. I am wearing baggy shorts, and the seat has already wedged them up so high that you can see my pasty white inner thighs. My fear was that if I cycled any faster...something might fall out.

"CYCLE! CYCLE! Come on, everyone. Let's encourage him," she shouted.

I bit my lip, mumbled to myself, "Ok you asked for it," and brought my legs up to speed. With every upswing of my legs, I managed to catch a full glimpse of my genitalia in the mirror on the wall. At one point, I felt a testicle pop right out of my shorts. I tried to slow down, but every time I lost rhythm, Sergeant Leather Skin would add five more seconds onto my sprint. Apparently, some of the ladies in the class got a kick out of the "sinusoidal peep show," thus making that minute feel like an eternity of embarrassment. I have decided to wear padded bicycle shorts to all subsequent classes that I attend, should I have the courage to return.

Soon enough, I will be returning home for the summer, where I can enjoy my real road bike as opposed to a stationary one. It is hard to believe that a second year of university is already drawing to a close. Unfortunately my plans for the summer are rather grim. I once again plan to spend the better half of my summer studying away in some dismal library.

SUMMER BREAK EDITION

SHELF LIFE

I am back in Montreal for the summer months, and I have spent my summer studying for the MCAT (Medical College Aptitude Test). The MCAT is an eight-hour exam that covers virtually every category of modern scientific knowledge and theory. It's a massive undertaking that requires months of studying. It has been said, "One needs a good head to become a doctor." That may be true, but I contend that more important than a good head is a good ass because of all the damn sitting and studying.

It's hard to believe that I have already been going through this routine for two full months. I have seen much improvement in my practice test scores but there is still work to be done. Unfortunately, we are approaching the wire, and like many of my colleagues, I am entering "Crisis Mode."

I was out grocery shopping the other day, when the first symptoms of the crisis set in. I was rummaging through milk cartons, checking the expiration dates when I noticed that the earliest date was August 14— test day. It was slightly unnerving to know that the time period between this very moment and the biggest test of my life had dwindled to the mere shelf life of a carton of milk. Rather than flipping out, I persuaded myself that I still had plenty of time by buying an expired carton of milk.

THE MILITANT LIBRARIAN

The library has once again become my second home, and I have come to realize how important proper library etiquette is. Last week while studying at the public library, my cell phone rang. So I wouldn't bother anyone, I answered the phone and began to walk toward the exit. There are two separate walkways, one for entering the library and one for exiting. The two walkways are side by side, separated by the librarian's desk. Absorbed in my call, I mistakenly walked out through the "entrance." A truly grave mistake as far as library infractions go. As my body passed through the threshold of the walkway, the librarian's head popped up from behind the desk. "You! Freeze!" she shouted.

She caught me by surprise. I turned with my hands above my head, as if to surrender. "You can't go out that way; you're going to have to walk back through, AND GO AROUND!" she barked. I was shocked. This was the kids' section. Would she have yelled at a toddler if he had made the same mistake?

"Are you serious? You actually want me to come back in and walk around?" I asked in disbelief. "I'm already outside." I was expecting to hear, "No problem, just don't do it again," but the librarian jumped up from her desk like a lioness ready to pounce. I was on her turf...and in the library, the librarian is king. I think this woman missed her calling. If it wasn't for her blind eye behind those huge bifocals, I'm sure she would have been sent to manage some military checkpoint in Iraq.

To avoid a problem, I submitted to her demands. I walked back in through the entrance and walked out through the exit just beside it. The whole ordeal took less than thirty seconds, but the frustration of submitting to a librarian in a power struggle lingers on...I could almost hear her mutter under her breath, "Librarian: 1, Student: 0," as I walked by.

Later that day, I decided to stop in at the grocery store next to the public library. Let me just say that nothing is quick at this grocery store. The average age of the shoppers is seventy-eight, the aisles are narrow, and the shopping carts are huge (because they double as walkers). Whether it was luck or fate, while walking through the tofu section, I found myself in a rather interesting predicament. An elderly woman decided to abandon her shopping cart mid-aisle, which constricted the flow of traffic down the aisle. As I pulled abreast of the abandoned cart, I noticed a familiar woman coming toward me. It was almost too ironic to be true, but it was the very librarian that almost strip-searched me a couple of hours earlier. I buried my head in the tofu so that she would not recognize me right away.

The militant librarian came to a halt just in front of my shopping cart. She seemed rather impatient and gave my cart a violent bump. I turned around and stared her in the eyes just long enough for her to recognize me, and then I said, "Oh sorry, you're going to have to walk back up the aisle and WALK AROUND. You can't go out this way." It was the perfect revenge; for those few seconds it was *my* aisle. I was the tofu king. I had managed to settle the score with the foul librarian.

But I suddenly felt ashamed. I was now equal to but no better than the librarian. I didn't want to become consumed by the very petty power struggle that I despise. I pulled my cart out of the way and let her pass. Oddly enough, giving up power felt even more empowering than exerting it, and I think we both realized it. As her carriage rolled by, I still managed to mutter under my breath, "Student: 2, Librarian: 1."

THE DEER BUFFET

I miss Eastern and my independent way of life, but truth be told, I love being home with my parents during the summer, especially at the cottage. They crack me up. My Muj and Fuj—as my sisters and I so amicably call them—have either been busy traveling, or gardening up at the cottage. My mother spends hours in her garden commanding my father where to dig holes or which weeds to pull out. Muj has also spent countless hours spraying every plant with some putrid concoction she has conceived, which she believes keeps the animals away. It keeps *me* out of the garden for sure, as the active ingredients are vinegar and rotten eggs.

Over the last couple of seasons, we have had several terrible deer attacks. During the wee hours of the night, herds of deer come and ravish the cottage garden of all its flowers. My mother, tired of hosting the "Deer Buffet," decided to apply for a gun permit. The same woman who refused to buy products tested on animals was now adamant about camping in her garden in camouflage and blowing the heads off every little Bambi that set hoof in her precious garden. Naturally, this scared the shit out of my father.

77

Given my father's obsession with buying gadgets over the Internet, he set out surfing for a deer solution. He found a company in North Carolina that specialized in building robots that detect deer and deter them by spraying a highly pressurized stream of water at their torsos. Apparently, these mechanisms don't just attack deer; within seconds of setting up the device, it sensed my father and attacked him. In a startled attempt to dodge the pressurized stream of water, my father tripped and landed face-first in the mud. By the time we rushed out of the cottage to see what all the screaming was about, my Fuj had been brutally assaulted by the Frankenstein scarecrow; he was soaked from head to toe.

RICKY'S RICKSHAW

My parents recently returned from a week's vacation in Ogunquit, Maine. I was sitting outside when their car rolled up. I was unable to immediately tell what they had bought, but I knew it was huge. The Jeep's trunk was held closed with bungees, and poking out of the sunroof were two long wooden shafts. My parents excitedly jumped out of the car, kissed me hello, and then showcased their purchase.

"Your father and I bought something wonderful. We saw it for sale and we couldn't resist. Ricky, open the trunk."

I looked into the car window, but all I could see was lots of warped, splintering wood and large steel wheels. My father proudly opened the trunk.

"It's a real antique, brought over from Paris at the turn of the century," he explained.

I was immediately consumed with laughter. My parents had bought a rickshaw, a small touring carriage intended to be pulled by a human instead of a horse.

The report that I now get from my youngest sister, up at the cottage, is that on really hot days, my father pulls my mother around the garden in the rickshaw so the spray from the deer sprinklers can cool her off.

SEMESTER 5 LETTER 1

The MCAT is now out of the way. I managed to enjoy a few days of recuperation, and now I'm back at my apartment at Eastern starting my senior year of college.

I'm not sure what possessed me to wake up early and watch the homecoming parade. It was cold and rainy, but I nonetheless stood among the other parade enthusiasts. The parade came to a standstill, and the Homecoming Queen stood up to bask in her glory. Without warning, the float began to move again. The Homecoming Queen lost her footing and was ejected from the float like a flying rag-doll. I don't recall if her body bounced once or twice upon hitting the pavement, but I do recall thinking, *I'm due to write a Rubin Review*. (For the record, only the girl's pride was hurt.)

I have been extremely busy since I returned to Eastern in September. I am running a university-wide campaign for Senate. Many of you at Eastern have probably noticed my campaign posters. I welcome all your support and encourage you to vote for me come the elections.

THE POO SHOE

The other day when leaving my apartment, I accidentally stepped in a fresh steamy pile of dog shit. I was walking quite hastily when my right foot gushed through it. Due to its consistency, every little crevice on the bottom of my shoe was filled with poo. I tried rubbing the shoe against the pavement and some tree bark, but nothing was coming out of the traction wells.

Soon after, I boarded the bus and totally forgot about the incident. My first class of the day was Developmental Genetics. The professor was lecturing about "*quasimodin*," a gene that causes Zebra rats to become hunchbacked. I had never heard of a hunchbacked rat before, and I was quite intrigued by the discussion, but my nose began to twitch. There was a terrible smell of fecal matter emanating from the girl sitting to my right. It was a putrid smell, and I quickly arrived at the conclusion that she must have shat her pants. I wasn't the only one to smell the accident. I could see some other people's noses twitching as well.

My next class was Medical Lab. As I took my seat, my nose once again began to twitch…the smell was back. I quickly glanced around the room looking for the girl, but she was nowhere to be found. It then occurred to me that the smell had been emanating from my shoe all along. How embarrassing. What if people thought…

Before I had the chance to rinse my shoe at my lab bench, the professor began the pre-lab lecture.

"Today, we will be starting a three-week-long experiment, wherein we will be isolating a particular gene from our own DNA," he explained. He then announced that a team of nurses would be coming in to draw blood from each of us to be used for the workup.

I am *petrified* of needles. All of a sudden, my heart began to race, and the sweat began to drip. I have no problem giving a cheek smear or a urine sample, but blood…that's a little intrusive.

Due to my phobia of needles, I once again forgot about the smell. I decided I wasn't going to be a baby. I would valiantly endure the needle. After all, I would be having it done alongside all my classmates, and none of them seemed overly worked up about it.

The nurses barged into the lab with their big needles, and I felt my stomach turn. Naturally, I waited until the very end to have my blood drawn, but the more I put it off, the more terrified I became.

Finally it was my turn. The nurse tied off my arm and sterilized the area over the vein. She then said to me, "You have great veins. I should have no problem *sticking* a vein on my first try." She then turned around to prepare the syringe. I thought, *Holy shit...sticking a vein, hell, I'm not STICKING around.* I jumped out of the seat and bolted away with my arms flailing in the air.

"Runaway patient!" the nurse screamed. All my classmates looked up at me scrambling away. It was as if I had seen a ghost; my face was pale white, and I had sweat dripping from my brow. I ran through the lab and out the exit with the smell of poo following close behind. Rumor has it, I was so frightened I shat myself.

THE JACK-IN-THE-BOX TEEPEE

My friend Sammy asked me to be a guest speaker for an after-school program for grades one through six, where she volunteered once a week. She asked if I would read the kids *Oh the Places You'll Go,* my favorite book, and stimulate a conversation about what we all want to be when we grow up. I happily obliged. Little did I know how difficult kids could be.

I showed up half an hour early with Sammy, and we prepared the room and a snack. Sammy suggested that since I was a "special guest," I should make a "special" entrance. In the middle of the classroom, there was a tiny teepee. Sammy persuaded me to sit in the teepee and then, on her cue, jump out and introduce myself.

When the bell rang, I quickly climbed into the teepee. It was really small. I had to sit with my legs and arms tucked into my chest. The kids started to slowly trickle in, and Sammy served them their snacks. Remarkably, the kids did not notice me. I sat and sat, but Sammy never gave me a cue. I listened to the conversation between the kids right next to me. Two boys were talking about ghosts. One of the boys claimed his dad had killed a ghost, while the other claimed ghosts weren't scary. A boy named James went on a tirade about how, if he saw a ghost, he would just laugh in its face. *Interesting,* I thought, *here I am in a perfect situation to test this boy's assertion.* All I had to do was stand up and the sheet that covered the teepee would make me as good a ghost as any.

Despite the temptation, I waited for Sammy's cue. After close to twenty minutes, I grew impatient and exploded out of the teepee like a Jack-in-the-Box, yelling, "SURPRISE!" Take it from me, James was all talk. He was so scared, he almost swallowed his tongue. The kids were stupefied. I yelled "SURPRISE!" a second time, but they all just stared at me with blank faces. It's not every day a full-grown man jumps out of their mini classroom teepee. I smelled a pungently familiar smell, but this time it wasn't from my shoe.

After snack time, I read the book to the children. Despite the incessant booing and the pieces of Lego they threw at me, I think I really got through to them. We formed a circle, and the children described what they wanted to be when they grew up. Most of the boys wanted to be soldiers, police officers, or assassins. The girls wanted to be hairdressers, teachers, or fashion designers.

There was also a little girl named Julie. She was just starting first grade, and she was no more than three and a half feet tall. "Julie, what do you want to be when you grow up?" I asked.

"I want to be a paleontologist, specializing in the Paleozoic era," she answered.

"Excuse me…" I gasped.

All the kids looked confused. "I think what Julie means to say is that she wants to collect dinosaur bones, right, Julie?" I asked.

"Well, not exactly, Mike," she answered. "I want to pick up anything that was fossilized between the Precambrian and the Mezoic periods, so that includes fish and plant life as well."

This girl seemed really bright. I was tempted to ask her if she knew anything about "quasimodin" and hunchbacked rats, but a piece of Lego hit me in the head, and I lost my train of thought. Kids these days…

THE CLAW

As an extracurricular activity, I decided to learn American Sign Language (ASL). I attend a three-hour class every week, which runs until the end of the semester. The classes are held in a small conference room on campus. I arrived just on time for the first class. As I walked through the door, I realized that the instructor had not yet arrived. About ten women sat around a long conference table staring at me as I walked in. Seeing that the only available seat left was at the head of the table (in front of the blackboard),

I sat there. I happened to be wearing a button-down shirt, and I was carrying a briefcase containing my laptop. The girls were still staring intently at me, so I decided to give them all a wave hello. Lo and behold, every girl waved back at me in exactly the same way. It took a second for me to realize what was going on. They thought I was the instructor. I reflected for a second...*pretending to be a sign language instructor is wrong*, but then I thought, *GO WITH IT*.

I then proceeded to lift my left hand and draw a loop through the air. Suddenly, ten hands were in the air doing the same thing. *Too easy*, I thought. I then did a medley of different hand gestures, and I watched them desperately try to keep up. It was awesome. I made them all do "The Claw," an ugly mauling gesture I can do with my hand because I am double jointed. I walked around correcting all those who didn't have it to my standard.

I was just about to write my name on the board when the real instructor walked in. I gave the class a final wave and moved my stuff away from the head of the table. The women seemed overtly embarrassed and annoyed. Luckily the instructor did not seem to notice that I had gotten the class warmed up for her.

The real instructor is an extremely interesting woman. She was born deaf, so she teaches the class only through signs and sometimes by writing on the board. In just two classes, I have already learned a tremendous amount.

During the last class, one of the girls fell asleep. BIG MISTAKE. The instructor did not appreciate that. She positioned herself directly in front of the sleeping girl and let out the most horrific sound I have ever heard: MRARPH MRARPH. After about five seconds of this dinosaur-like cry, the sleeping girl's head popped up in total confusion. The instructor then proceeded to reprimand the girl using sign language. I didn't completely understand what she was saying, but I understood that if the girl fell asleep again, she would be kicked out. Oddly enough the signed warning was loud and clear.

SEMESTER 5 LETTER 2

It's that time of year again when the leaves have finally fallen off the trees and the days have become so short it seems like it's always night time. Sometimes I will pop my head under my halogen desk lamp and pretend that it's still the middle of the summer, and I'm out on my cottage dock, tanning. My daydream is usually interrupted by the horrible smell of singed hair. On the upside, my parents bought me a beautiful new winter coat. It's a huge puffy coat, which completely covers my body from head to toe. I was skeptical of it at first, because I felt as though it made me look fat, but enough people have convinced me that this is not the case. Then again, I don't think anyone would honestly say that the coat makes me look like a giant marshmallow.

HELL WEEK...WHEN THINGS LOOK BLEAK

This semester is proving to be the most grueling of my time spent here at Eastern. The heavy amount of schoolwork, compounded with my new positions on the University Student Council and my newly elected position on the University Senate has left me with little time to spend on writing or flash mobs. As is the case with most secret societies, Borissio's leadership position has been handed down to the next worthy candidate. I am ok with it, now that my newly-elected seat on the University Senate enables me to directly champion student causes and sentiments with the highest level of university administration.

I guess a good place to start would be "Hell Week." Hell Week can be likened to a rare eclipse, when the essay schedule crosses over the exam schedule and all forms of natural light become obscured. Over a period of eight days, I had seven exams and three papers due. I did not see the light of day. Classes were no longer about mastering interesting concepts, but rather rote memorization.

My Developmental Genetics course became a nightmare. Because Genetics is a fairly new science, it lacks a functional nomenclature. Rather than referring to chemicals by their molecular formulas, geneticists chose the most outrageous names and sounds to describe their newly-discovered "morphogens." Cerberus, Chondroitin, or Goosecoid are a few examples. My professor actually discovered "Beta-Ratenin," a crucial molecule in the development of Zebra rats.

In the past decade, my professor's research has gained much support from the Zebra-rat-obsessed zoological community. He has published half a dozen journal articles on Beta-Ratenin, alone, which has earned him the title, "Father of Beta-Ratenin." Despite how fascinating his Zebra rat research might be, he often fails to capture his students' respect due to his patronizing demeanor.

Developmental Genetics was the last of my exams during Hell Week. I was ill, burned out, and unreceptive to memorizing stupid terminology—and my grade on the exam reflected those realities. I decided that since the grade was uncharacteristic of my abilities, I would write my professor a letter explaining the predicament that had led to the weak grade. He responded with a short but pompous e-mail, which read, "Tough luck."

I decided to pay the professor a visit. I figured he didn't know me by name and, maybe, if he realized who he was talking to he would show some compassion. After all, my name and face had been all over the campus news as a result of the recent University Senate elections.

His office was a temple of self-worship. All his published articles were framed on his wall. He quickly identified me as one of the "keeners" who never missed a class and frantically wrote down every word he said. He was shocked to learn that I was the same Michael Rubin that had bombed his midterm. I once again explained to him that I had just come off my Hell Week, all the while conducting a university-wide campaign for Senate.

He reclined in his armchair and began a self-indulgent speech, which he must have given at least a million times before. "I too was an undergraduate student, and a Masters student, and a PhD candidate...Want to know the key to my success?" He leaned forward and whispered, "BALANCE. Why yes, balance is the ticket. Don't take on things you can't handle, and do the most important things first!"

It was kind of ironic that I was being lectured on balance from a guy who spent his whole life in a lab dissecting rats or trudging through shit-infested Guatemalan sewers.

"I have met too many 'Mike Rubins' in my day," he continued. "People who take on more than they can handle and spread themselves too thin. I see this often with junior faculty members. Young, eager people, willing to always accept more responsibility without any concept of what they are realistically capable of handling, and you know what happens to them?" he asked.

At this point, I didn't want to hear his answer but he volunteered it anyway. "THEY FAIL."

He was baiting me; he wanted to upset me. "Well, Sir, essays have deadlines, the election date was beyond my control, and you refused to offer an alternative make-up date for your exam," I refuted.

"But you didn't have to run for Senate," he interjected.

I didn't have to take a stupid class on Zebra rats either, I thought.

The professor was known to gain pleasure by flustering students, and boy was he good at it. I can only imagine how many times students went running out of his office after having been leveled by his condescending demeanor. As if my grade didn't bother me enough, this pompous jerk was trying to make me feel like a total failure.

NO! I will not have this, I thought. Then a brilliant idea popped into my head.

I looked him straight in the eyes and said what he had probably never heard from a student before. "Sir, you are absolutely right...I don't think I have planned my time effectively. Your course is my priority."

Dr. Zebra Rat gave me a confused look. He was totally perplexed. Usually by now, students were running out of his Beta-Ratenin shrine sobbing.

"In fact, I'm looking for someone to help me schedule my time and develop time-management strategies geared toward my life goals. Someone intelligent and experienced who can devote himself to helping me get my life back on track, someone who is critical, but truly wants to see me succeed." I leaned over the professor's desk and asked, "How would you like to be my mentor? I would love to learn from your experience. I could come in twice a week and, together, we could review what I am 'realistically capable' of achieving. You can help review all my important day-to-day decisions."

The professor was speechless; his intimidating, anger-provoking tactic had failed. He looked totally stunned and nodded ever so slightly. I could tell he was thinking, *Shit, what have I just gotten myself into?*

"Perfect," I said. "I have a class to catch, but I will stop in tomorrow so we can schedule additional times to meet. I hope with your help I can refrain from 'spreading myself too thin.'"

Over the remainder of this year, I plan to systematically manipulate this professor. He has already started to treat me differently than his other students. I think he may be frightened of me, because I was impervious to his intimidation tactics. I hope that by the end of the semester, I can get him to reweigh my final exam grade so that my bombed midterm will count for less.

THE BUS RIDE MEDICAL EXAM

The bus continues to be a source of entertainment for me. One morning as I rode to campus, an old couple boarded the bus. I was sitting up front on the middle seat of a three-seat bench. Despite the entire bus being empty, the old couple came and sat down on either side of me. It was odd to say the least. The weirdest part was that it didn't even seem to bother them that I was sitting smack dab between them. They continued to talk to each other as if I weren't there. The woman must have been hearing impaired because she kept yelling "What, what, what?" which prompted the old man to lean closer to me to speak to her. He was practically lying across my lap yelling into her ear.

The couple was very cute. But they were invading my personal space, there was a pungent smell of mothballs, and the man had terrible breath. Every time he opened his mouth, there was a putrid gust of air. It was a harsh olfactory mucous smell that could only be attributed to chronic sinusitis.

I eventually piped up and said, "Sir, would you like to switch seats so that you can sit closer to your wife?"

He gave me a good long smile, then slapped his hand down on my leg and squeezed my inner thigh. "I have been sitting next to that old bag for sixty-five years; it's about time I sit next to someone else," he said jokingly. His laugh seemed to circulate a lot of stinky air in my direction. I held my breath, but the rancid smell still managed to seep into my nostrils.

"Son, I'll bet you're going to the university?" he said.

His wife did not hear the question (nor the comment) and continued with her incessant "What, what...?"

"Yes, Sir," I said in an extremely low voice, because I barely had enough air left in me to speak.

"What are you studying?" he asked.

"Medical Science," I answered.

"Thank God, a doctor. We need more doctors!"

Before I had a moment to correct him, he was already listing everything that was wrong with him. He informed me that he suffered from terrible sinus problems, even though I had already arrived at that conclusion myself. He opened his mouth as wide as he could to show me his inflamed tonsils. I cringed and tried to look away, but he demanded that I take a closer look.

"Sir, I am really not qualified to examine you..." But he insisted that I check it out. It looked as if he had two slimy white ping-pong balls lodged in the back of his throat. I concluded to myself that those were probably the source of the rancid breath. He went on listing all the things that were wrong with him. He even tried to get me to feel his wife's goiter. Fortunately, we arrived at my stop just as he moved onto complaints about his prostate and his trouble urinating. The bus might not be as efficient as a car, but the people I meet are certainly more entertaining than the radio.

HOW TO IMPRESS THE HEARING IMPAIRED

Recently, while riding the bus home from campus, I noticed a group of deaf women sitting at the back of the bus. I was intrigued by their conversation. By this time, I had already attended a half-dozen sign language classes, and I had mastered some of the basic elements of conversation. From what I understood, they were talking about shopping at the mall. I was intrigued by the fluidity of their motions and the dynamic of their group conversation.

I tried to be discrete, but they eventually realized I was watching them. One of the women signed to the group, "Check out that 'cute' guy staring at us from the front of the bus." Actually, I wasn't sure if that was exactly what she had signed, but it seemed plausible. I immediately became very excited. I felt the need to explain to them that I was one of them, that I too could sign.

This would be my first attempt at applying what I had learned in the course. Without thinking, I signed, "My name is M-I-K-E." They did not seem overly impressed; everyone at some time or another learns how to sign his or her own name.

I decided to step it up a notch. I tried to sign to them, "I am not deaf, but I am learning to speak sign language." Only it didn't seem to come out as planned. I ended up saying something along the lines of, "You are deaf, but I speak sign language." That sure as hell did not impress them.

I automatically went into a cascade of signs that I had rehearsed a hundred times in class. "I am a student taking American Sign Language at the University. I still need a lot of practice."

One of the girls served as the spokeswoman for the group and carried on a short, simple dialogue with me. After asking and answering a few simple questions, I had already exhausted my working vocabulary. I decided to return the earlier compliment. I signed to them that they were all "cute." I mimicked the exact sign that they had used to describe me. Surprisingly, they all seemed offended by the comment. I was at a loss for words, or signs rather. The bus was becoming full as we neared my stop. Luckily, a crowd of people moved in front of me and this temporarily severed our line of communication. I tried to use the brief intermission to think of something intelligent to sign back to them. The only words that I could think of that had not yet been used were barnyard animals, rooms in a house, and colors.

As the bus approached my stop, I became desperate. *Think of something smart*, I thought. I walked to the back exit of the bus and signed to them the first thing that came to mind. "I would love to stay and practice, but I must give my white dog a bath." I don't know what possessed me to say that, seeing as I have no dog, but at least it came out as a proper sentence. For some reason, the girls burst out laughing. I considered that a good sign.

Later on that evening, I was reflecting on the conversation, and I decided to look up a couple of the words. I quickly realized that the girls had laughed at the end because I had mixed up the sign for a dog with that of a horse. I also learned that the sign I had thought meant "cute" actually meant "fat." No wonder they were so upset when I tried to compliment them. But why had they described me as fat in the first place? It soon dawned on me that I was wearing my new coat on the bus. The girls must have mistaken the puffiness for blubber. Proof that the jacket did in fact make me look portly. If you happen to see me walking around campus, and I look a little more stout than usual, do me a favor and keep it to yourself, it's the *coat*!

DRIVEN BY AN ANGEL

Night class had let out a little later than usual, and I had just missed my bus home, which only comes around every half hour. I had opted not to wear my new puffy jacket that day, feeling too self-conscious, and I sat there at the bus stop shivering in only a jean jacket. I was miserable and cold. All I wanted was a ride home.

I stared up at the sky as if to ask God, "Why can't anything ever just go smoothly...Do you hate me?" I was having a rough day and the thought of waiting in the freezing cold angered me. Then, almost as if God had answered my prayer, a bus emerged in the distance. As the bus approached, I noticed it didn't have the usual "Richmond 6" title in front. This one read "SPECIAL." I immediately assumed that this bus was out of commission and I took a couple of steps back from the curb.

The bus pulled up next to me. The door opened, and the driver yelled, "Where you headed, buddy?"

"I want to go downtown...are you the Richmond 6?" I asked.

"Nope...I'm done my shift. I'm taking her into the garage. Where is it you are trying to get exactly?"

"I'm trying to get home: the corner of Richmond and Kent, right beside the new club, Mack's."

"Well, hop in, I'll take you there. I'll make it on my way."

I thanked him and boarded the bus. For once, I had my own personal bus. It was the quickest bus ride down Richmond I have ever been on. He didn't stop at a single stop. Then the bus turned down Kent Street and dropped me off at the entrance to my apartment. It's not every day a public city bus drops me off at my front door. Something was indeed "special." I sincerely thanked the driver and asked him if he was an angel. He winked at me and said, "Don't mention it; just return a kind favor to someone else should the opportunity arise." He waved goodbye and the special bus disappeared into the night just as it had appeared.

THE NARCISSISTIC PROFESSOR

I dreaded meeting with Professor Beta-Ratenin. Sitting with him undoubtedly meant an hour of belittlement and a lesson in egotism. I have always dealt with narcissistic people in the same way: by avoiding them. Unfortunately, I needed my final exam grade re-weighed and I would endure whatever abuse was required to convince him to do so.

I knocked on his office door and found him sitting at his desk. He motioned for me to come in. Just as I sat down in front of him, he picked up the telephone and dialed out. I'm not sure who he was speaking to, but he scolded the person on the other end of the line. I tried to tune out, and forget that he was wasting my precious lunch hour.

After about ten minutes he put down the phone, propped his legs up on the desk, and asked:

"How can I help you?"

I reminded him that I had come to discuss time management strategies.

He let out a phony chuckle and said, "Indeed, you have come to an expert on the matter. I could have never achieved all that I have today without discipline and organization. Fortunately, those are characteristics impregnated into my character. Some people just can't handle all they desire to take on, and they have to settle for doing less. By the looks of your midterm exam you should probably reconsider your involvement in everything other than studying."

"Sir, I do take on a lot, but usually not more than I can handle. The reason I am here is because I did become overwhelmed and it is highly uncharacteristic of me," I explained.

He motioned for me to pass him my Eastern University agenda book. "Let me see what kinds of activities are keeping you busy." As he flipped through my daily planner it became evident how much of my recent time had been absorbed by my new position as a University Senator.

At the last Senate meeting, I had been nominated to fill vacant positions on multiple senate subcommittees, some of which I turned down immediately, others I felt it my duty to consider. The Dean of Science approached me personally and invited me to fill a position on the University Animal Care Council (UACC), a subcommittee he chairs. The role of the committee was to oversee and investigate all matters pertaining to the ethical use of animals for research at Eastern. I figured it was a noble cause, and who was I to turn down my Dean?

As the professor browsed through my agenda he took note of all my senate-related meetings. He seemed to pay particular attention to an upcoming UACC meeting.

Suddenly his demeanor totally changed. He took his feet off the desk, looked over at me with a grin and handed the agenda book back to me.

"It seems you are involved with many things... They appear to be important things. It is vital that students take an active role in University governance." Was he showing signs of empathy? Was he having a stroke?

"I was just about to make a glass of tea, can I interest you in a cup?" Was he trying to poison me?

"No thank you, not a tea fan."

"Often students come to me complaining about their poor grades and I find out they were out boozing at some party the night before the exam."

"Sir, I assure you that was not the case..."

He seemed to take a minute to ponder the situation. "In all honesty the midterm was a challenging exam, over eighty percent of the class failed. I will re-weigh the final for the entire class. I will make the announcement tomorrow."

I was in shock. What had I done or said that miraculously turned this pompous jerk into a compassionate human being?

Soon after, he dismissed me from his Beta-Ratenin shrine. I walked out totally perplexed. I was happy that I had achieved my goal, but I was not really sure how I had done it.

Several days later at the University Animal Care Council meeting it became overwhelmingly obvious what had transpired. Dr. Beta-Ratenin's lab was under review. A recent lab visit had raised some concerns about animal welfare and he was now under investigation by the UACC. Either in hopes that I would help him, or in fear that I could hurt him, he had become empathetic to my request. How the tables had turned: I would now be on a panel presiding over the future course of his Zebra rat research, his life's greatest accomplishment.

For a few moments I enjoyed the thought of having him squirm before me pleading for a second chance for his precious rats, but finally I opted to step down from the panel on the grounds that I had a conflict of interest. But if he treats his lab rats as poorly as he treats his students, he is in for some "tough luck".

SEMESTER 5 LETTER 3

THE MEDICAL MUSICIAN'S ACCIDENTAL CONCERTO

Many of my professors are medical doctors. Often a professor will be "on call," while lecturing, and it is not uncommon for them to be paged during a lecture. Usually, the professor's beeper will vibrate and she will excuse herself from the class for a minute or two, then she returns and class resumes. This happens fairly routinely.

Eastern is an extremely technologically-advanced university. All the lecture halls have wireless access for Internet as well as audio. Professors are given tiny little wireless microphones that clip to their shirts and broadcast directly to the classroom's speaker system. This allows the professor full mobility during the lecture. Not being tethered to a speaker system by a wire has its benefits, but it has its shortcomings, as well.

Not too long ago, during one of my classes, my professor suddenly clenched her side. She then told the class that we would have to excuse her for a moment, as she had something urgent to attend to. I assumed her pager had vibrated, and she was being summoned to a phone or a medical emergency. The class remained seated but a lull of chatter filled the lecture hall. The professor left in quite a hurry.

I began speaking to a friend sitting next to me, only to be interrupted by the sound of a giant *fart*. It seemed as if everyone had heard it; it came from all directions. The room became silent; everyone looked around for the guilty culprit. Right when people started holding their noses and blaming Gilbert, who had been known to toot his horn on occasion, BOOM! Another huge fart resonated through the lecture hall. But where was it coming from? It sounded as if it was coming from all four corners of the room.

"That wasn't me! It's coming from the speakers," Gilbert yelled, amidst the escalating laughter.

Our professor was obviously tending to a sudden personal emergency; unfortunately, the washroom was still in range of the wireless network.

I don't know what professors eat nowadays. Based on the sounds, I assume baby food or rotten ice cream. It was a true concerto, hundreds of people sitting in seats, paying good money only to hear a soloist pass air through a tube. I was hysterical, I couldn't breathe. Some people refused to breathe. Other people were so grossed out, they left. The professor went on tooting for another minute or so, and then ended the symphony with a grand flush.

A roar of laughter filled the room. When our professor walked back into the lecture hall she was greeted with a standing ovation.

THE FOOD-BANK TRUCK

Every year, my fraternity holds a food drive to help stock the Ithaca food bank for the winter season. This year's food drive was a huge success. Our fraternity canvassed over three thousand households in the Ithaca area and collected over ten tons of food. It was a beautiful, sunny day, and all who participated had a great time fulfilling a noble cause. For the first time in my tenure with the fraternity, I was able to witness a complete packing of the eighteen-wheeler truck on loan to us by the food bank.

This was no small vehicle; it was a moving truck. We managed to pack it to the brim with non-perishable foods. It was hard work collecting the food and packing the truck, but knowing our efforts would feed hundreds of hungry families made it all worth it.

The only problem was that the truck was parked at our fraternity house, and we needed to get it to the food bank that evening for processing. Unfortunately, no one had a truck-driver's license. Among the racecar drivers and fighter plane pilots we had in our fraternity, no one seemed to know very much about driving large trucks. We held a small meeting to decide how to get the truck to the food bank. The fraternity had promised the food bank ten tons of food that evening, and they were going to receive it—on time!

Then Little Bert came forward. "I'll drive it," he said. "Last summer, I worked construction and I learned how to drive a dump truck." We immediately made him captain. Little Bert is one of the fraternity's youngest members. It seemed highly counterintuitive to let him commandeer the truck, but we had no choice. Spence, the organizer of the food drive, was designated as his co-pilot. Don't ask me why, but I was nominated to fill the third seat in the truck.

I should have realized from the outset that we were in trouble when Bert put the truck in reverse instead of drive. Although I must admit that once he got the truck rolling, he maneuvered it quite well. He was actually driving perfectly—until we had to start switching gears.

Once we hit the freeway, the terror began. Bert couldn't figure out how to get out of fifth gear. In a desperate attempt to downshift, Bert engaged an "overdrive function." The truck started roaring down the highway like a bat out of hell. The RPM spun out of control, and the truck began "red lining." There was a terrible grinding sound coming from the engine. I was convinced that a cylinder was going to explode and the pistons were going to shoot right into the passenger compartment and impale us. An awful smell of grinding metal emanated through the vents, and every emergency light in the old truck was flashing.

"Bert, what the hell...I thought you knew how to drive trucks!" I shouted.

"Well, the guy I worked with last summer made it look so easy."
This was not the response I was hoping for.
"You mean you've never driven a truck before?"
"No. How could I? I only recently got my license!"
Spence and I were so terrified we ended up clutching each other.
"Bert, if we survive this, I am going to kill you myself," I threatened.

I rolled down the window to signal other vehicles to get the hell out of our way, and we honked the horn to warn everyone that we were approaching. I had a terrible mental image of the truck rolling over with thousands of canned fruits and packages of pasta strewn across the highway.

We eventually managed to slow the truck down and opted to continue driving well below the speed limit. Our slow moving, rattling truck with flashing hazard lights attracted the attention of a highway patrol cruiser. As if there wasn't already enough anxiety, we now had a police car on our tail. The cop ordered us to pull over. Bert brought the truck to a halt safely on the side of the road.

Technically, we had not done anything wrong, but explaining the situation to the officer could be complicated. The officer was immediately suspicious of what three young men were doing driving an eighteen-wheeler at a snail's pace along a major highway. His skepticism immediately evaporated, once we opened the truck to reveal the ten tons of nonperishable food donations. The officer was so impressed by our efforts that he provided us with a police escort all the way the food bank.

In the end, we successfully delivered the goods relatively on time and thankfully lived to tell the tale.

SEMESTER 5 LETTER 4

THE LIBRARY STAMPEDE

My preferred location of study during exam period is on the bottom floor of the Eastern Medical Library at cubical 184. Cubical 184 is one of twenty cubicles that run along the northern wall of the library. Legend has it that this cluster of cubicles is blessed, and anyone who sits there will be able to study from morning to night without ever having to get up. Naturally, these twenty seats are the library's prime real estate. Each cubical is located at the end of an aisle of bookshelves that span the length of half a football field. These long aisles of books serve to buffer noise and prevent people from walking through the area, thus making the northern wall the most reclusive location in the entire library.

Obviously not everyone is privileged enough to sit along the northern wall. There are other choice areas to sit in the library, as well. There is always a vibrant Jewish community on the second floor. Groups of Arabic students choose to study at tables in the computer section. Asian communities often sprout up in very enclosed or confined areas. There are also some areas that are less conducive to studying, areas where the desks are broken, light bulbs are missing, and garbage is rampant. The engineers usually dominate those areas. On any given day, students can go to the library and choose any one of the seven hundred library seats that appeals to them. This all changes during exam period. The library becomes way too overcrowded—a game of survival of the fittest. Those who don't arrive before 8:00 a.m. lose out on prime real estate, and by 10:00 a.m., even the slummiest areas are taken over.

Latecomers will often roam around for hours waiting for a seat to vacate. Some people opt to just claim a piece of floor and lie there for hours studying. This past exam period there was a near tragedy because a group of Asians established a study group between a set of bookshelves that electronically compress to occupy less space. Someone searching for a book entered the specific call number into the nearby computer and, as the shelves began to electronically move and compress, a pack of scared Asians came running out from between the shelves screaming for their lives.

I usually get to the library for about 9:00 a.m. By that time, most of the good desks are taken and I have to settle for the densely-packed, small-cubicals section. This area is the low-income housing of the library. The desks are less than an arm's length apart. If the person next to you has bad breath or body odor, you smell it. It's not a safe area. If you leave your desk for an extended period of time, chances are, when you get back, your light bulb will have been stolen. Studying there usually didn't bother me. Once my earplugs were in and the books were open, it didn't really matter; I just studied.

One afternoon, my concentration was broken by an annoying clicking sound. Even with my ear plugs, I heard the annoying CLIP, CLIP, CLIP; the sound was very familiar, but it couldn't be what I thought it was. Who would have the audacity to clip their nails in the middle of the library? There was another huge CLIP and a piece of a toenail landed on the page I was reading. Sure enough, the girl next to me was sitting there clipping her toenails! "Disgusting," I muttered, as I tried to maintain focus.

Eventually, the clipping stopped and she took out the nail file. That did it for me. There was no way I was going to sit there inhaling her toenail dust. I was completely revolted! I think I might have even gagged once or twice at the thought. I quickly threw my stuff into my bag and stood up. The woman shot me a dirty glance as if to say, "Stop rustling around, you're disturbing me." I just stared right back at her and said, "*Pig*," and walked away.

It was now clear what had to be done. I had to get to the library early enough to secure one of the secluded seats on the northern wall. The next day, I awoke bright and early and arrived at the library fifteen minutes before opening. A crowd of thirty had already amassed and was waiting quietly by the library entrance. Nobody uttered a word. I obviously tried to break the silence.

"Early bird gets the *book* worm," I joked. Nobody seemed too receptive to my comments. People started scowling at me, so I shut up and waited silently.

At exactly 8:00 a.m., a librarian unlocked the door. The group of gunners suddenly came to life. People started pushing and shoving through the door. Before I could even grasp what was going on, my body was plowed like a rag doll through the entrance of the library.

Once inside the library, the pack of people began to walk relatively quickly. Confused, I did the same. Suddenly, the walk turned to a trot and then a full-out gallop. I was now running alongside thirty other people through the mezzanine of the library, and I had no idea why. All of a sudden, the herd split; half the people ran toward the eastern stairs and the other toward the western stairs. I chose east.

I realized what was going on. Everyone was racing for the northern wall cubicles. I was in the middle of the pack as we entered the stairwell; I had to pick up the pace if I wanted a spot. The good news was there were still another three flights of stairs to go. You might not be able to tell by looking at me, but I am quite fast on the stairs.

It felt like we were running away from a bomb. People were yelling and screaming; there was no sense of community. Everyone was out for him- or herself. Suddenly, a girl at the front of the pack slipped and tumbled down four stairs. The binder she was holding opened up and all her papers went flying through the air. I stopped at the bottom of the stairs to see if she was all right. The girl looked up at me. I still remember the look of defeat in her eyes. I wanted to help her, but another girl beside me grabbed me by the arm. "There's no time; let her go; you still have a chance."

I jumped five stairs at a time to pull in front of the pack. When we reached the basement level, those individuals who had taken the other stairwell were already emerging on the opposite end of the floor.

Apparently, people in that stairwell slid down the banisters, though I did not see it with my own eyes. The adrenaline was pumping, and I ran faster than I ever had in my life. It was like a track and field race. The bookshelves formed perfect track lanes. I sprinted down the sixth lane. Between the books, I could see the heads of my rivals bumping up and down as they sprinted next to me. One guy a couple of lanes away, grabbed books off the shelves as he ran so he could reserve as many cubicles as possible. One girl threw her knapsack from ten feet away to reserve her desk. I even saw one girl do a flying dive to secure the chair she wanted.

Victory! I managed to capture cubical 184, my favorite seat in the whole library. There was a brief moment of neighbors congratulating one another on their successful captures, and then everyone resigned themselves to their studies. I placed my earplugs in my ears and cracked open my books, only to be overcome by a laugh attack. The absurdity of what had just transpired finally registered. In a completely empty library of seven hundred seats, a small group of keeners felt the need to duke it out for a select few seats.

THE TRUE SPIRIT OF CHRISTMAS

The next day, I opted to study at home. In the afternoon, I became very sleepy, which is often the drawback of studying in the comforts of home. I decided to take a walk down the street to Starbucks to get a coffee. Upon leaving the apartment, I was unaware that something would happen on this walk that I would remember for the rest of my life.

It was a perfect winter day; huge snowflakes fell from the sky. All the stores were playing Christmas tunes, and families were skating in the park. Mobs of people were walking around shopping for the holiday; Christmas spirit was in the air. I happened to walk past a man sitting on the steps of a shop. Upon seeing me, he jumped to his feet and summoned my attention.

The man startled me. He had quite a frightening appearance. All his teeth were missing, and the lower half of his face looked caved in. His body was ill and gnarled, as if he had been suffering from a chronic disease. He was shorter than I and fairly hunched over. From a distance one would think he was an old man but, from up close, his eyes revealed he could be no more than a couple of years older than me.

"Sir, can you give me a dollar so that I can buy a coffee? I need to buy a coffee. I need a dollar to buy a coffee," he stammered.

His words were slurred. He was not drunk; rather, he showed signs of being mentally challenged or having suffered from a degenerative disease.

"Yes, I have a dollar," I responded, as I reached into my pocket.

The shopkeeper must have thought he was harassing me and came running outside. He looked at the poor man and yelled, "For the hundredth time...please leave! Or I am going to call the cops."

He looked at me and explained, "I'm sorry, he has been sitting here all day and hassling all my clients. I'll call the cops and have him taken away."

I looked up at the shopkeeper. "No need to call the cops, we were just leaving."

I asked the man if I could treat him to a cup of coffee at Starbucks. He was quite skeptical of the offer but he eventually obliged. We walked down the street together, and I quickly realized that the guy was completely paranoid. He asked me a battery of questions. He had noticed that I was wearing a pair of scrubs and wanted to know if I had been sent by the hospital. I reassured him that I was a student and I had no intentions other than to buy him a coffee and chat.

We walked into Starbucks, and the man picked out a seat for us. I went to the counter and ordered two large coffees. The man yelled to me that he wanted a "double double." People sitting in the coffee shop stared at him and probably wondered what the association was between us. I took the coffees to the milk station, and I carefully added two milks and two sugars to both coffees. I mixed both coffees thoroughly, because I hate when the bottom half is sweeter than the top. I then wiped down both cups and brought them to our table.

I handed the man his coffee and sat down beside him. He looked up at me with huge tears in his eyes.

"Is everything alright?" I asked.

"Everything is perfect! You just made my Christmas. I watched you make my coffee, and you did it with such love and care. For once, somebody treated me for what I am…a human being. Thank you; it's the best Christmas gift I could get."

He put out his hand and I shook it. He held it as hard as he could for half a minute, as if he never wanted to let go. I felt like I had just won the largest lottery. My small act of kindness had elicited a response of unforeseen magnitude. This man had in turn made my holiday season. I sat and chatted with him for half an hour about nothing in particular. I returned to my desk feeling completely spiritually revitalized.

SEMESTER 6 LETTER 1

I have received the proofs of my graduation photos. I have provided documentation to the Registrar's Office proving my middle name is "Ellery" and that I didn't request it to appear on my diploma merely as a joke. Barring I don't screw anything up, I am set to graduate with an honors degree at the end of the semester. Rather than focus on how my stint at Eastern is coming to an end, I will dedicate the last and final volume of the Rubin Review to going out with a BANG. This semester has already yielded some hysterical moments, which I hope I can do justice to with my writing. Without further ado I present to you the final volume of the Rubin Review.

THE THRONE OF THE SCORPION KING

It all started the night I returned to Eastern after Christmas vacation. I had spent the entire day on the train with very little to eat. That evening, I arrived at my apartment famished. The pantries were bare aside from a pack of saltines and a vat of prunes. It is common knowledge that exceeding the six-prune limit in a period of twenty-four hours could have detrimental effects, but hunger prevailed. I sat there eating prune after prune until eventually the vat was empty.

At times, I could go for a number of days without having to use the facilities. Although some may consider this extremely unhealthy, it has served me quite well considering my phobia of public toilets. The morning after eating the half-kilo of prunes, I was sitting in class, and inevitably my stomach began to gurgle. Suddenly, I felt the entire contents of my bowels liquefy and rush toward my sphincter. I clenched hard, but I knew I could only contain the force for a short time—certainly not enough time to take the bus home. I excused myself from class, hoping to God my sphincter's hold would not fail as I climbed over the people sitting next to me.

The gurgles seemed to come more and more frequently. Violent bowel contractions were indicative of an imminent expulsion. I ran down the corridor, hunched over in search of the nearest washroom. I pushed through a set of heavy doors that led me to the Department of Entomology in the Life Sciences building. Luckily there was a washroom adjacent to one of the labs.

I quickly began covering the toilet seat with toilet paper using the Octagon Technique I had developed in my first year in residence. I had gotten to my fifth layer around the seat when my defenses began to fail.

The sound of heavy rain pummeled the inside of the bowl. Then, like the eye of storm, there was dead silence and everything was tranquil... except for a faint rattling sound coming from the corner of the stall. In that corner, to my astonishment, there was a small scorpion shaking its tail and watching me.

At first I thought I was hallucinating; after all, I had lost a tremendous amount of body fluid very quickly. As the deadly creature began to approach me, I became convinced of its authenticity. Its beady eyes stared me down, and it was poised to sting with its poisonous tail. *A scorpion in the middle of winter? Impossible!* I thought.

But its existence was entirely plausible. After all, I was in the Department of Entomology. Maybe he had escaped from a nearby lab. I tried to shoo the evil creature away, but it continued to approach, poised to attack. I threw a ball of toilet paper directly at it, but that didn't seem to deter it from coming closer. "LEAVE ME ALONE," I yelled, but the venomous creature continued to advance. He was within a foot of me as I sat there, fused to the can. Having my pants down around my ankles put certain restrictions on using my feet as weapons. I flailed my arms and legs like a madman in the hope of scaring the pest away.

Then I remembered a TV show I had seen about armadillos. Armadillos pray on scorpions and snakes. If I could somehow mimic an armadillo, maybe I could scare the scorpion away. I had little choice; no one was likely to walk into the washroom and save me. I remember learning that armadillos swallow lots of air and inflate themselves like balloons, only to burp it out slowly. They also make snorting and squeaking sounds typical of most nocturnal predators. I began to burp and squeak.

My idea seemed to work as the sounds sent the creature scampering away. By that point, my business was just about done, as the little monster had literally scared the shit out of me. I finished up as quickly as possible. I wanted to get out of there before the scorpion reappeared.

I made the mistake of trying to flush all five layers of toilet paper down in one shot. As I washed my hands, the toilet began to overflow and ooze all over the floor. I looked back only to find the scorpion floating belly up in the water. Let that be a lesson to all scorpions. When I sit on the throne, you had best treat me like the Scorpion King!

SEMESTER 6 LETTER 2

THE JAWS OF LIFE

A couple of weeks ago I had a terrible mishap at the grocery store. Mitch and I have been known to cause trouble each time we go grocery shopping together. In the past, we have been reprimanded for sword fighting with frozen fish, using the grocery P.A. system to locate each other, and even tooling around in the motorized carts reserved for the handicapped—but everything pales in comparison to the most recent incident.

The episode started off as a dare when Mitch challenged me to sit in the child seat of the shopping cart.

"Hey FAT ASS, I bet you can't sit in the baby seat of this shopping cart," Mitch yelled.

"I bet you I can," I refuted.

"A steak dinner says your ass is too big," he challenged.

I have always prided myself on having a small ass. I knew it wouldn't be comfortable, but I was convinced I could fit.

"Watch me," I said, as I leaped into the shopping cart and forced my legs through the little squares. It was a *very* tight squeeze, but I managed to do it.

"See, I told you I can do it!" I said proudly, as I sat in the child seat with my legs dangling down through the holes. My crotch was squished up against two metal bars, and the metal around my thighs quickly began to cut off vital blood flow to my legs, but the feeling of triumph made it all worth it. Before I had any time to contemplate getting out, Mitch grabbed the handle of the shopping cart and began to push me up the aisle at a lightning fast speed.

"STOP! STOP! Let me out. This is breaking my NUTS!" I howled, but he continued to push me up and down the aisles smashing the cart into random objects. The pain was excruciating. I felt like I was sitting in a giant nutcracker.

He then pushed me into the fresh produce section and abandoned me there. I felt much like I did as a child, when my mother would leave me sitting in the shopping cart while she went back to get something she forgot from a previous aisle. Only now, I didn't have a diaper padding my wiener. My legs were too short to reach the ground and there was nothing nearby to grab onto.

What I never realized as a child, but quickly caught onto as an adult, was that if you swing your legs back and forth you can actually propel the shopping cart forward. After a couple of minutes of nut cracking, leg-swinging action, I managed to get myself over to the orange and apple section. I grabbed onto the counter in a desperate attempt to pull my body out of the carriage. As I shuffled around, I triggered a fruit avalanche. The apples began rolling off the display. Luckily, I was able to swing the shopping cart around and catch them in my cart. It quickly became apparent that there was no way to lift my body out of the shopping cart, unless I took the weight off my crotch.

I swung my legs forcefully back and forth, until the shopping cart began to do wheelies. Finally, with enough momentum, my feet landed on the floor. I was standing hunched over, my butt still wedged into the seat of the cart. The metal bars fused with my crotch prevented me from standing erect. The shopping cart was resting on its two rear wheels with the two front wheels dangling up in the air.

I shuffled up and down the aisles searching for help. After a couple of minutes, it was no longer funny. I seriously needed help. I certainly didn't appreciate everyone's laughter as I strolled by. I was losing sensation in my lower limbs.

I trudged passed two Russian men who began to laugh hysterically and began to converse in Russian. I said, "What are you laughing at? Is this your first time shopping in America? This is how you're supposed to do it. Get with the culture! BORSCHT, AISLE FOUR."

I eventually attracted the attention of several cashiers and the manager. I was in severe distress and wanted nothing other than to be removed from the cart even if that required having the fire department cover me in lubricant or cut me out using the Jaws of Life.

The store employees began to help me. They emptied my cart and helped lay me down on the floor. Mitch pulled on one of my arms, and a feisty cashier pulled on the other. I did a porpoise-like squirming action and, before long, I was freed from my metallic trap.

The manager gave me a stern talking-to. After such a painful experience, the last thing I wanted was to be lectured to like a child. I'm almost a university graduate for heaven's sake. He basically told me that the seats were designed for children and there were other accommodations that could be made for grownups who are unable to walk and shop. He then asked if I had any other questions about the grocery store, to avoid future mix-ups or hazardous incidents.

I apologized for the mishap. I then looked at Mitch and back at the manager and said, "I do have one question. Can you show me your most expensive cut of *filet mignon*?"

LET'S GO STREAKING

I have stopped going out to clubs in Ithaca because, unless you get in before 9:00 p.m., you have to stand in a two-hour long line. All the little Eastern chicks dress up in their mini-skirts and halter-tops and stand in these lines freezing their asses off, until the stupid bouncers deem them worthy to enter. I am opposed to it socially and economically. Wouldn't it just make more sense if customers were inside buying drinks rather than waiting out in the cold? Needless to say, I refuse to go out to a club if I have to wait in line for longer than ten minutes.

Anna wanted me to take her to Mack's. Since its opening in November, Mack's had become the Ithaca "hot spot" and it was conveniently located right next to my apartment. At times, the line to Mack's was so long it virtually stretched to the lobby of my building.

Intent on beating the line, Anna and I set out to Mack's at 9:00 p.m., and we walked right in. The club was completely dead; we looked around, had a drink, and then decided to meet up with a couple of friends at a bar down the street. We figured that since the club was empty, we would have no trouble getting back in. On the way out, I informed the bouncer that we would be back shortly. He gave us a quick stare-down and a nod.

A half hour later we were back at Mack's. The club was probably still empty but a massive line had formed outside.

I walked up to the bouncer and asked him to let us back in.

"Sorry, buddy, you'll have to go to the end of the line," he said.

"What? I just stepped out a couple of minutes ago. You honestly don't remember me? I'm not waiting in the huge line to get into an empty club. I was just inside."

It was absurd. Clearly the guy recognized me; he was just being a prick! "This is small town America not fuckin' Hollywood. Blow off the whole image thing and let me and all the other freezing customers into the club so your boss can make some money," I protested.

I like to think I make an impression when I meet people. Clearly, I hadn't left a lasting impression on this guy. The bouncer absolutely refused to acknowledge that he had let us in earlier. "Get to the back of the line before I put you there," he threatened.

"Screw this…There is no way I'm waiting in the freezing cold so that the club can maintain an image," I said, as I grabbed Anna and stormed off.

Anna and I were both a little upset that a meathead bouncer had curtailed our night at Mack's. It was freezing cold, and we opted to head to my place and relax in the hot tub.

By the time we made our way down to the hot tub, we had already completely warmed up. That's when we decided to go roll around in the snow so that plunging into the hot tub would feel even better.

It was freezing outside. I was only wearing boxers and flip-flops, and Anna was sporting her underwear and bra. From the door of my building, we could see all the people still waiting pointlessly outside of Mack's.

"Hey, Anna, do you want to run up to the entrance of Mack's and give the bouncer a reason to remember us?"

Seconds later, the two of us were sprinting toward Mack's wearing only undergarments. "LET US INTO MACK'S, LET US INTO MACK'S!" I wailed.

We quickly earned the respect of the hundred or so individuals waiting in line.

They cheered us on and yelled out words of encouragement. Most of the people had become disenchanted with standing out in the cold, and my mockery of the bouncers galvanized the group.

As I ran beside the people in line, slapping them five, one of my flip-flops got wedged in the snow. I put my bare foot down into a patch of ice, and the shock of the cold sent violent contractions up my leg. Before I knew it, I had lost my balance and ended up head first, bare-chested in a heap of snow. The crowd loved it. They cheered even louder. I quickly jumped back to my feet and continued taunting the bouncer.

It was the same bouncer as before, and I stood in front of him in my underwear, covered in snow.

"Hey, dude...do you remember me? We were inside earlier; you wouldn't let us back in...BIG MISTAKE!"

I then climbed up onto a mound of snow. I turned toward the line, which had now become a very loyal audience.

"Are you cold? Are you sick of waiting? Well guess what...this club is empty. They are keeping you outside to create an image," I yelled. "I refuse to be used as an advertisement on my weekend...or anytime. I am not a puppet. I want a drink, and I want it NOW! Screw Mack's! Let's go to Tonic! there is *no* line there."

All it took was one person to step out of line, and the bulk of the people jumped on the bandwagon. A mass exodus began from Mack's toward Tonic a block down the road.

I winked at the bouncer. "Now, will you remember me?" I then grabbed Anna and raced back to my nice warm hot tub.

SEMESTER 6 LETTER 3

THE AIRPLANE STORY

A couple of weeks ago I flew to Montreal for an interview. On my return flight to Ithaca, I had a relatively long layover in the newly-built Toronto airport terminal. It is a state-of-the art facility with moving floors and flat screen plasma TVs. I found my gate, took a seat, and pulled out my computer to do some work. I was astounded that there wasn't a single electrical outlet anywhere around the gate. I searched the entire end of the terminal, but there wasn't a single plug to be found. It seemed kind of odd, given that the terminal was so modern and built to service business passengers.

I began to roam the airport in search of a plug and eventually found one on the opposite end of the terminal. The plug was in a weird spot. It was probably intended to power a vending machine. I became extremely frustrated because my computer power cord was too short to stretch to anything I could potentially sit on. There happened to be a vacant wheelchair nearby, so I wheeled it over and sat in it while I worked. I hung all my carry-on bags on the back of the chair, and I sat there with my legs in the stirrups doing my work. I was comfortable and focused and I must have lost track of time.

About an hour later, I happened to glance down at my watch and noticed how much time had elapsed. I was far away from my gate, and

I had no idea when my plane was scheduled to board. I called out to an Air Canada employee who happened to walk by.

She immediately scurried over to my wheelchair, and I handed her the ticket. "Excuse me, Miss, can you tell me when my flight to Ithaca is set to board?"

She looked at the ticket, then at her watch. "Oh shit! Your plane has already boarded. We need to get you to your gate STAT!" she gasped.

Before I could say anything, she unplugged my laptop, grabbed the handles on the wheelchair, and began pushing me full speed through the terminal. It was a fairly awkward situation. I wanted to show her that I could walk there by myself, but we were already moving too fast for me to jump out of the chair.

"It's ok, Miss, don't feel obliged to push me. I can walk there by myself," I said.

"Now is not the time to be proud. Your gate is far away. You'll get there a lot quicker if I push you. You haven't got any time to lose; hopefully we can still get you on your plane," she said. "You will be flying to Ithaca on a Dash-8; it's a small plane, so we'll have to find a way to transport you onto the runway. Unfortunately, there's a tremendous amount of snow accumulation, so we can't push wheelchairs outside. I'll have to radio for a specialized motorized car to pick you up and take you from the gate to your plane."

This had become an extremely awkward situation. I had been labeled as a cripple, and my inability to rectify the situation truly turned me into one. How does one explain, while being pushed in a wheelchair, that he or she is not actually handicapped? I figured it would just be a lot simpler if I went with it. Soon enough, I would be flying out of Toronto and, in all likelihood, I would never see this woman again.

When we got to my gate, I was able to see the last few passengers outside on the runway boarding the plane. The airport personnel began closing the rear compartment and were taking the protective sleeves off the twin propellers.

I sat anxiously in the wheelchair at the threshold of the gate waiting for a motorized car to pick me up and take me the few hundred feet across the runway to my plane.

The airport employee seemed nervous but kept reassuring me none-theless. "Don't worry. We're going to get you on that plane. The trans-port should be here any second now." I sat there helplessly watching my plane prepare for departure without me. Was I really going to miss my plane just to avoid a little embarrassment?

The last passenger had now boarded, and the ground crew was pre-paring to remove the steps. There was no motorized vehicle in sight and it did not look like my plane was going to sit there waiting for me.

I looked at the anxious airport employee who was still mildly out of breath. I had no choice. I leaped to my feet and grabbed my bag off the back of the chair. She had a perplexed look on her face. I felt awful, but I looked at her and said, "It's a miracle, I can walk!" and then I sprinted toward the plane. Several of the steps had already been removed, so I took a flying leap through the door. I looked back at the gate, and she was still standing there in utter disbelief. I gave her one last wave and went to go find my seat.

CONTROL THE BEAST BETWEEN YOUR LEGS!

A while ago I decided to take up horseback riding. My friend Brooke and I found a lady on the outskirts of Ithaca who agreed to give us semi-private lessons. The woman was eager to take Brooke on as a student, since she had past experience, but she was hesitant about me since I was a beginner.

Several weeks ago, Brooke and I set out for our first lesson. It was a relatively short drive out of Ithaca into farmland. I was really excited; I had always wanted to learn how to ride. At times I imagined myself as a "cowboy" sitting atop a giant, muscular stallion. I even brought my camera along to get a picture of me riding the giant beast.

We pulled up to a small farmhouse surrounded by stables and barns. It was eerie and cold, but in the distance, we saw a large well-lit arena. The farm was dead quiet, but the strong smell of animal assured us that there were definitely lots of horses in the vicinity.

We found the woman in the barn, and she interviewed us briefly. She wanted to make sure that she "connected us to the right horse based on our ability and personality." She then led us into a stable that housed several dozen horses. First, she took us to the horse she had selected for Brooke.

It was a beautiful black mare with a shiny mane. I was in awe of her size. She had robust legs and defined musculature. She was truly an amazing creature. Her name was Missy, and Brooke was instructed to brush her down, clean her up, and saddle her for riding.

The lady then took me to the other end of the stable to introduce me to my beast. Her name was Sadie. She was an old, white, decrepit, five-foot tall pony with a sagging belly.

"Sadie is an excellent pony to learn on," the instructor assured me. "I usually teach small children to ride on her. I hope she will be able to hold your weight." I pretended not to be upset, since I didn't want to hurt Sadie's feelings, but I was expecting a larger, more masculine horse.

I was afraid I would break Sadie's already curved spine if I sat on her. I figured we would have a better chance of getting anywhere if Sadie climbed on my back. The lady began her instruction with me. Apparently, there is much that has to be done before you can even mount the horse. The instructor taught me how to brush the horse, put on its saddle, and even how to pick up its poop and clean the crud from between its hooves.

I guess it was while I was cleaning Sadie's rear left hoof that we began to bond. Looking at Sadie's short and relatively round physique I realized that the two of us really weren't all that much different. After all, we both loved carrots.

Mounting the pony was terrifying, I was sure she would buckle under my weight, but she held strong. Initially I felt high and powerful until I was dwarfed by Brooke on her giant horse. Riding was easier than I had expected. Sadie was an excellent listener and followed my instructions perfectly. The instructor taught me the basics of riding and emphasized the importance of being in control of my pony at all times.

The few times I let Sadie decide where we were going to go, the instructor reprimanded me. "CONTROL THE BEAST BETWEEN YOUR LEGS!" she yelled. Once I had mastered the art of trotting, I was taught to "post." Posting trot is probably just as much work for the rider as for the horse...pony. Within minutes, I had mastered the *up-down, up-down* motions, and the instructor complimented me for having "an excellent sense of balance and a natural ability to ride." I attributed my success to Sadie for being so cooperative.

Toward the end of the lesson, Brooke asked if she could "gallop." Galloping, for those of you non-equestrian folk, is full speed on the horse. The instructor gave her permission but suggested that I refrain. I was content just trotting around and resting my sciatica from an hour of heavy pounding.

Brooke commanded Missy to gallop when she was right alongside me. Sadie must have thought the command was for her, and she began to accelerate. My pony went from virtually zero miles per hour to a full out gallop in less than three seconds. I was terrified. Who would have thought an old pony could travel at such a lightning-fast speed?

My feet instantly fell out of the stirrups, and my body started bouncing around uncontrollably. My stout little pony had become Hidalgo in an attempt to surpass Missy. Within seconds, I was catapulted off Sadie's back like a projectile and bounced twice upon hitting the ground.

I had trouble getting out of bed the next morning. Every muscle in my back and butt had stiffened up. I almost wished that I could be seated in a wheelchair and pushed around by a kind airport employee the whole day.

THE PINK FLAMINGO SUIT

After declining a nomination to run for president of the University Student Council, I was recruited by another presidential nominee, Mark Ogorski, to endorse his campaign. I became one of many campaign managers on the "Ogorski" campaign team. The final day of campaigning fell on Valentine's Day, and I was among the handful of campaign members assigned to the University Community Center.

I arrived on the scene bright and early. We set up our campaign booth, put on our campaign T-shirts and began giving out flyers and candy. Soon, the costume we had rented for the day arrived. It was a giant pink flamingo suit.

We thought a flamingo was an appropriate mascot, since the Ogorski campaign color was pink and it was, after all, Valentine's Day. Unfortunately, the guy who had volunteered to wear the costume never showed up. It was a tremendous waste of campaign resources to just let the costume sit there, but where were we going to find someone animated, impervious to humiliation, and willing to parade around as a giant flamingo?

I had no choice but to do it myself. Once dressed up, I was roughly nine feet tall with a wingspan of six feet. It quickly became apparent that nobody could identify who was inside the costume. It didn't take long before I realized how potentially entertaining the flamingo suit could be. The costume was heavy, and each time I tripped and fell down, I needed two or three people to hoist me back onto my feet again.

It was really hot inside the bird, and I began to sweat profusely. Hallucination due to heat stroke became my excuse for my actions. Eventually, the costume began to take over. I *became* a flamingo. When I saw friends, or attractive girls, I would run over and hug them. Costumes impart a free invitation to hug anyone you please.

You really learn a lot about your friends' true personalities when they don't know it's you. I made one of my friends hold my wing and help me down a flight of stairs. He was more than happy to help, even without knowing it was me. When we got safely to the bottom, I gave him a big hug and thanked him personally by name.

"How the hell do you know my name?" he asked, completely freaked out.

"The Ogorski Bird knows all," I chirped and tried my best to fly away.

I was probably having a little too much fun with the costume. I ventured into the university fitness center and into a step class. The instructor thought I was a riot and invited me to the front to help lead the class.

I then moseyed into the cardio center. All the people on the treadmills and stationary bikes were perplexed to see a giant pink flamingo working out alongside them. I stepped onto a treadmill and began a light jog. It didn't take too long before one of my giant webbed feet got caught, causing me to lose balance and fall on my face. I ended up pinned between the treadmill and the back wall with my huge flamingo head continually banging against the back wall as the treadmill continued to run. The whole gym was hysterical, and people had to actually jump off their exercise machines to help me up.

My last stop was the Community Center day care. There is a large window for parents to watch their kids play. I thought the kids would enjoy seeing a giant flamingo. All it took was one kid to yell "Monster!" before widespread fear and hysteria spread through the daycare. In hindsight, I realize that to an unsuspecting tot, a giant flamingo costume can just as easily be interpreted as a child-eating pink alien.

By the time I had made it back to our booth, the costume volunteer had shown up and I was more than happy to turn over the sweaty costume to him.

THE REVERSE SURPRISE PARTY

I am generally not an enthusiastic birthday person. Birthdays simply remind me of how responsible and independent I should be. Birthday cakes remind me of wishes that have not yet come true. There is much stress for the birthday person, who always has to be alert and wary of the unexpected surprise party. However, this year was different. I had an amazing idea that made my birthday an exciting experience.

A couple of days before my birthday, Anna asked me if she could throw me a birthday party at her apartment. My first response was obviously, "NO! I don't want a birthday party…"

"Oh well…I should have just planned a surprise party, don't know why I even bothered asking you," she said. "Seeing as it's too late for me to plan a surprise party, are you sure you don't want to invite a few friends over for drinks? You'll be sorry when you celebrate your birthday alone."

Suddenly, a diabolical scheme popped into my head. My eyes must have lit up because Anna said, "Good, I knew you would reconsider."

"Actually, I have," I answered. "I would like to have a surprise birthday party."

"How can you have a surprise party if you know about it?" Anna asked.

"That's the twist," I explained. "I could reverse the surprise onto all the guests attempting to surprise me." Thus the idea of The Reverse Surprise Party was conceived.

The reverse surprise was executed as follows. Anna invited all my friends to my surprise birthday party to be held at her apartment. I made it very easy for everyone to keep the secret by telling them that Anna had invited me to her apartment for dinner on my birthday, but afterwards I would appreciate if everyone could meet us downtown for drinks.

On my birthday, I went over to Anna's apartment early under the auspices of going to the library to study. I helped Anna prepare the apartment and the dinner. We had found a large clean cardboard box and we brought it up to the apartment and placed it in the corner of the living room.

Before my guests were scheduled to arrive, I climbed into the box and Anna covered it with some books and magazines. The box didn't exactly go with the apartment's décor, but it did not look out of place. It certainly seemed harmless. No one expected me to be sitting inside it.

All my guests showed up on time. From inside the box, I listened to them talk about me. Once I was certain that everyone had arrived, I silently dialed Anna's phone. She pretended to have a conversation and warned all the guests that I would be at the door in roughly five minutes.

Everyone quickly scampered to hide in the corner of the room, around my box. The room was silent. I could hear all my friends breathing in anticipation, mere centimeters away. I heard Anna turn on the video camera and then she gave the code phrase, "I think he's coming."

I jumped out of the box, yelling "SURPRISE!" There were many frightened faces, a lot of screaming, and a multitude of uncontrollable flailing arms. It was an extremely successful "reverse surprise." It took everyone a couple of seconds to catch their breath and process what had just happened. But most people agreed that it was a truly memorable surprise party. I hope the reverse surprise party will grow in popularity so that, soon, birthdays will be a source of fear for everyone and not just the individual growing older.

COLUMBUS – THE PET I ATE FOR DINNER

Did you know that grocery stores sell pets? Not just bunnies. A while back I was shopping around the seafood section when the lobster tank caught my eye. I figured lobster would make for an interesting meal. I inquired as to how one might cook lobster and was told that lobsters must be boiled for twenty minutes before they can be eaten.

Simple enough, I thought, and bought one of the midsize crustaceans. Apparently, lobsters can live without water for more than two days, so there was no pressure to cook it immediately.

I placed the lobster in a makeshift confinement cell...my bathtub. I watched him for a while, as he explored his surroundings. He had an inquisitive personality, so I named him Columbus. I spent much time that day watching Columbus. He had many adventures. He attacked the soap, discovered the drain and left a brown residue at one end of the tub. When dinnertime came around, I boiled a large pot of water and prepared Columbus for his hot tub. I found a recipe on the Internet that read:

Place the live lobster head first into the boiling water. Do not be alarmed; it is normal for the lobster to scream once submerged in the boiling water. Although lobsters have a nervous system, their pain receptors are primitive, and their death is probably painless.

I stared down at the sweltering water. *I would scream too if I was placed headfirst into boiling water*. I held Columbus over the pot, and the steam caused him to go into a frenzy. I began to feel as though this wasn't going to be the swift painless death it was made out to be. I couldn't bring myself to drop him in. I refused to murder an innocent creature in such an inhumane way.

After a couple of minutes of deliberation, I decided to return Columbus to my bathtub. I guess that is how Columbus acquired pet status. To make a long story short, I did indeed end up cooking him. I was uncomfortable showering in front of a sea creature with powerful pinching claws. What if he got hold of a loosely hanging body part? Then, his shell began to turn black. He needed nutrients and concentrations of salt that only seawater could provide. Realizing that Columbus was doomed to death either way, I worked up the courage to boil him. I think Columbus would have preferred it this way. He made a delicious meal and his memory will always live on inside me.

SEMESTER 6 LETTER 4

THE CANNULATED ARTERY

A while back, I was visiting Brooke in her office. She works as a researcher in the University Psychology Center and conducts many psychology experiments for the department. Brooke was busy preparing an experiment, while I was sitting at her desk checking my e-mail.

I knew that Brooke was expecting a subject for her experiment, and I promised her that I would leave as soon as the subject arrived. To earn credits for the course, the department requires all first-year psychology students to participate in several psychology experiments over the course of the year. They are usually simple but tedious experiments that involve identifying shapes, colors, or letters.

The subject showed up, and I was able to tell just by looking at him that he was a freshman.

"Is this SSC room 807?" he asked.

"That's right. Are you here for the experiment?" I asked.

He nodded to give a definite yes. I should have called out to Brooke to let her know her subject had arrived. But an amazing opportunity had just presented itself. For that brief instant, I was the psychological researcher...context is everything.

"Did you fast this morning?" I asked. I grabbed a pen and clipboard off the desk and pretended to make notes.

"No? Was I supposed to? Nobody told me…"

I quickly cut him off. "Well, usually we require our subjects to fast before they undergo a *surgical procedure*…"

"SURGICAL PROCEDURE?" he gasped.

"Yes, today we will be cannulating your right femoral artery to measure your arterial pressure during the experiment."

His face turned white, and he muttered, "But…this is only worth one credit."

He turned and bolted down the hallway. I obviously found this very funny. Brooke, on the other hand, did not. She thought the unnecessary psychological stress might skew the results, plus she was the one who had to go running after him.

THE TOILET TALKER

Last week was once again fraternity initiation week. Initiation is a weeklong process during which time the whole chapter traditionally wears suits and ties on campus. Personally, I don't mind dressing up; it makes me feel smarter. What I do mind is explaining the true reason for my attire to everyone who asks me. I usually throw out a quick "presentation," "interview," "meeting," or "funeral" to save my breath when the question comes up. The ladies at the coffee shop actually believed I attended a different funeral every day of the week.

"It must have been a mass stabbing," one of the coffee shop ladies commented, as I walked away with my coffee.

The suit actually helped me avoid a potentially embarrassing situation this past Thursday. I arrived at my afternoon class a couple of minutes early, set down my stuff, and headed for the washroom. I always use the faculty washroom since the "student washroom" is never as clean. I have been using that washroom for months and never once have I been caught by a faculty member.

I opened the door slightly to make sure no one was inside, checked the hallway to make sure the coast was clear, and then entered. I was at the urinal when I heard the door open. I turned my head in the opposite direction to ensure that the incoming professor could not see my face.

"Hey, Doug," the professor said, as he passed me by and walked into a stall.

"Hey," I muttered back. Big mistake.

"Great presentation you gave this morning. I have been meaning to drop by your lab for a quick chat," the professor said.

Oh no, the professor must have thought I was "Doug" because of the suit. This guy was a toilet talker; he didn't seem to mind sputtering from both ends at the same time. I had to get out of there fast before he realized that I wasn't Doug—or worse, that I was a student.

I quickly washed my hands. The toilet talker suddenly ripped a roaring fart. I couldn't control myself; I burst out laughing.

"Sorry, Doug," he muttered.

From my seat in class a few minutes later, I could see the washroom door. Oddly enough a man in a black suit with a full head of hair just like mine had just entered the washroom. My guess is his name was Doug and he was in for a rather awkward encounter.

SEMESTER 6 LETTER 5

The semester is winding down and, subsequently, my career as an undergraduate student is drawing to an end. I have finished all my exams, and barring any unforeseen disasters, I will be granted my honors degree in Medical Science in June. My last month as an undergraduate student has been busy.

MIKE VISITS THE MORGUE

My Forensics Pathology professor is head of the Pathology unit at the University Campus Hospital. He felt it would be a fitting complement to his lectures to have his students come on a tour of the hospital autopsy suite. I have seen several cadavers over the last couple of years, but I have never had the opportunity to actually go down to the hospital morgue. One evening during the last week of class, the professor offered to take us down to the morgue to bring to life all that we have learned about death.

We followed our professor into an elevator in the east wing of the hospital. We began our descent into the bowels of the hospital. The autopsy rooms were not as I had imagined. It was a newly renovated facility with an upbeat color scheme, bright lighting, and beautiful chrome paneling. One of my colleagues even commented that she wanted a kitchen with the same décor.

However, the room gave me the creeps. It made me uncomfortable knowing that human remains were laid out on the gurneys and their body fluids drained onto the floor as their carcass was butchered like a cow at a slaughterhouse. The instruments were frightening. They did not look anything like those found in the operating room; they looked more akin to medieval torture tools. If you weren't dead at the start of the autopsy, you certainly would be soon after some of those tools cracked through your skull.

Our professor then led us into the hospital's body storage facility. It was just like in the movies: a huge refrigerated filing cabinet with bodies that slide out on gurneys. The room was small, and all of us were packed tightly together facing the twenty-four little storage compartments that each housed a cadaver. The room was chilly and a little eerie, so it didn't bother me that all of us living people were huddled together. The professor slid one of the compartments open and we all watched in awe.

Suddenly, a loud sound came from behind us. We now know that it was the compressor on a piece of refrigeration equipment, but at the time, it seemed entirely plausible that it could have been a ghost or a zombie.

All of our bodies were pressed up against each other. All it took was one girl to shriek, which elicited the propagation of an unstoppable loop of terror. The girl's shriek frightened all of us, especially the guy next to her. The guy's arms flapped which startled the girl on his other side, which caused her to let out an even louder shriek. In this manner, fear was propagated throughout the group like an electric current. The whole ordeal took place within a matter of seconds. The initial sound didn't scare me; it was the sharp elbow to my ribs, caused by a thrashing arm that sent me reverberating. Even the professor became frightened, let out a screech, and slammed the storage compartment shut. It was a vicious cycle of fear with everyone's delayed reaction continuously re-frightening everyone else. We were all screaming and flailing our arms; we couldn't control it.

After we all regained our composure, we decided never to speak of the incident again and continued on our tour. We were then brought into a specimen storage room. This room had thousands of jars all neatly organized in compact shelving. As I peered into the shelves, it became apparent that the samples were organized by body parts. Imagine looking at a shelf with over a hundred bottled human brains. I couldn't help but think that each of the brains had a name and, at one point, contained a wealth of information. It was one of the most disturbing field trips I have ever been on.

ACCEPTANCE SPEECH FOR THE MODERN GENTLEMAN FRATERNITY OFFICER OF THE YEAR AWARD[1]

Dear Parents, Alumni, Fellow Brothers, and of course, beautiful dates,

Welcome.

New guys…Congratulations!

I would like to take this opportunity to thank my brothers for this meaningful award. I would also like to dispel some common misconceptions our parents may harbor about fraternities, as well as let you all know how much this fraternity means to me.

There are some stigmas associated with fraternities. I guess because they are slightly secretive, people often feel that fraternity boys are always up to no good. Movies usually portray the stereotypical "frat boy" as beer guzzling, bone-headed, wild animals, but you would be hard pressed to find anyone like that in this room…we prefer guzzling *rye*. I contend that we are a different breed of fraternity men. People are astounded to learn of some of the amazing things we do.

As the outgoing Academic Officer I am delighted to inform you that we participate in many educational activities. This semester we held a fraternity book talk. It was an extremely engaging event, even if the book under discussion was by Dr. Seuss.

We are not just a group of friends who sit around drinking beer, surrounded by sorority girls, though that does seem to happen a lot. We are an *academic* society, as well as a social group. We go on educational field trips in an attempt to increase our knowledge and understanding of the world we live in. This

---

1   My goose story was inspired by a book I read that year, *The 7 Habits Of Highly Effective Teens* by Sean Covey.

past semester, we took a field trip to one of Ithaca's most historic sights, the Labatt Brewery! It was astounding how many members took part in this highly educational event. I remember mostly everything the tour guide said, up until my fifth free sample.

When I told my father three years ago that I was planning to join a fraternity, he let out a small chuckle and warned me to run as fast as I could if I ever saw a goat. Well, I assure you that there are many strange rituals associated with our fraternity, but none of them involve goats. Four liters of goat's milk maybe, but no goats.

Frat boys are always portrayed as a dangerous pack of wolves or hyenas, nocturnal predators always on the prowl for an innocent little lamb. Not true! We Modern Gentlemen are more akin to a flock of innocent Canadian geese, easygoing creatures that enjoy lounging around in warm pools of water. Sure, once in a while a goose may have an urge to scavenge amongst the leftovers of a party—and in some rare instances even share their findings with a friend—but for the most part I would say we are harmless.

Have you ever seen a flock of geese heading south for the winter? They fly in a V formation. By flying in formation, the whole flock can fly 71 percent farther than if each goose flew alone. Apparently, when a goose flaps its wings, it creates an updraft for the goose that follows, thus making it easier to fly faster for longer.

Similarly, as individuals, we all contribute to the community in our own ways, but as a fraternity we have contributed in ways that none of us could have achieved individually. This year, we collected over ten tons of food for the Ithaca food bank. Our efforts fed hundreds of families over the holiday season. We could not have accomplished this without teamwork and cooperation. Now that is something to be proud of.

I don't know how this was scientifically proven, but the geese in the back of the V honk to encourage those in the front. Our fraternity is truly full of HONKERS! We were the loudest fraternity on campus, cheering for our pledges when they won the dance competition this year. Whether it is a university election, a sporting event, or a fashion show, the fraternity always comes out to encourage its members.

Did you know that when the lead goose gets tired, he will rotate to the back of the V and allow another goose to take on the lead position? Division of labor. The fraternity works on the same principle. Different brothers "spearhead" different activities so that the most capable brother is always leading the flock.

Amazingly, when one of the geese gets sick or is wounded and falls out of formation, two geese will follow it down to help and protect it. They will stay with the injured goose until it is better or it dies.

Just the other day, one of our brothers wrenched his back playing football. Sure enough, two brothers swooped to his rescue and carried his fat ass halfway across Ithaca and up to the fourth floor of the fraternity house to lay him in bed.

Not so long ago, a couple of brothers found themselves in a rather inhospitable circumstance. Their safety was compromised. Within minutes of learning of their situation, a flying V of support swooped in, honking, and drove the assailants away.

By sharing in on another's draft, taking turns in the lead position, honking encouragement to each other, staying in formation, and watching out for each other, the flock accomplishes so much more than if each bird flew solo. As a fraternity, we have enjoyed this very same level of synergy.

As a fraternity, we have learned that one plus one doesn't necessarily equal two; it can equate to way more. This is the type of math you can't learn in the classroom but can only learn through experience, working and interacting with others. I may be graduating university with a degree this year, but I contend that a large portion of what I learned here at Eastern was through my involvement with this fraternity.

I have learned about different cultures, I have learned about teamwork, I have learned about leadership, I have even learned about some of the not-so-pleasant aspects of business.

For that I am thankful.

Seventeen of us are set to graduate at the end of this semester. However, I am confident that next year will be one of the best years that this fraternity will ever experience. The outgoing executive has worked hard to restructure the chapter, and I am proud to say that I have complete confidence in the future leadership of this chapter.

For those of us who are graduating, I hope we can all stay in touch and continue to see one another at formals to come. I will truly miss all of you.

Before I end, I just want to thank all the parents—in particular my parents, who flew down all the way from Montreal to come see what this fraternity is all about.

Thank you.

SEMESTER 6 LETTER 6

Packing up my apartment was difficult, both physically and emotionally. For two years, I worked hard to organize, clean, and decorate the apartment, and then within the span of a few hours, I ripped it all apart. I worked around the clock packing and wrapping items for the move. As always, at 4:00 a.m., the noisy recycling truck pulled up below our balcony and began to empty the bottles from the restaurant below. That truck has woken me up three times a week for the past two years. When I first moved into the apartment, the rattling of bottles and shattering of glass used to drive me crazy. I complained to the restaurant as well as to the city, but to no avail. "It's not our fault that you can hear the trucks," they responded.

Seeing as it was our second-to-last night in the apartment, Mitch and I ran to the fridge, pulled out a carton of eggs, and had our retribution for two years of ruined slumber. "It's not our fault if eggs happen to fall from the sky…"

THE DISMEMBERED SPIDER

It is a weird adjustment returning home. My parents are much the same as when I left. They still engage in the same ridiculous bickering. The other day, I listened to them argue about the best way to kill a spider.

My dad is not very good at killing spiders; he often knocks them off the wall and then loses them. This makes my mother even more frantic because "a spider on the floor is worse than a spider on the wall." This time, he wasn't taking any chances; he pulled out the vacuum cleaner and sucked it up. My mother became very upset. "Now the spider is going to lay eggs in my vacuum! Open the vacuum and make sure it's dead," she ordered.

My father obviously believed that his spider-catching method was foolproof and argued that the inside of the vacuum was an inhospitable environment for an arachnid to lay eggs. "In all likelihood, the spidy was probably dismembered as it was sucked up through the vacuum hose," he protested.

They stood there arguing over the fate of the spider in the vacuum for several minutes, while I listened, laughing in my room.

They have certainly aged since I last lived in their house. My father has finally decided to get contact lenses; only he has a terrible fear of touching his eyeball. To put in the contacts he requires a slew of mirrors, a full bottle of saline and dead silence for a full hour. My mother often has to help him by holding his eyelids open. The yelling and screaming that goes on is unbearably funny.

I am happy to be reunited with my family and friends, but I miss Ithaca and all the friends I made there. I get to go back in a couple of weeks for convocation, so the finality of leaving has not yet registered. When I return to Eastern in June, I am sure everyone will still be up to the same old. I hope by then that the new fraternity puppy will be potty trained and will have stopped drinking from the fishbowl with the hairy dead fish at the bottom.

CLOSING REMARKS

I received my grad pictures and they are not half bad. Along with the huge blow-ups of my face, there are several dozen wallet-size pictures. I never understood until now why new graduates feel the need to distribute pictures of themselves wearing the stupid gown.

For those of you who have not yet graduated, let me explain. The pictures simply serve as a notice for family members that you are a university graduate. The graduation getup prompts them to acknowledge that you are an intelligent individual, finally worthy of sitting at the "adult table" during family functions. Not to mention the photo usually fetches a modest cash reward.

I look forward to starting the next phase of my education at a new university, but I will miss Eastern terribly. Eastern has enabled me to take on many different roles, while always staying true to myself. I have packed the last three years with tons of adventure, and I wouldn't trade it for the world. I have made some unbelievable friends and learned a tremendous amount about life and who I really am. Not to mention I also earned an honors degree.

Varsity athlete, Leader of the Secret Society, fraternity executive, Senator, and member of the University Student Council, I have done a lot. I remember pulling up to Eastern on my first day, wondering how I would fare, and now I leave confident that I have left my mark and consider Eastern home.

I have tremendous Eastern pride, and it is tough to leave a place where I felt so comfortable and connected. I am sure that with time I will succeed and find adventure wherever life takes me next.

I just want to thank my readers, some of you who have been reading since the first issue and others who have joined along the way. If it weren't for all your positive feedback, I would never have continued to write.

I hope you have all enjoyed reading as much as I enjoyed writing.

Thank you.

Sincerely,

Mike Rubin